THE GREATEST TRADE

THE
GREATEST
TRADE

How Losing It All
Became Life's
Biggest Blessing

STEVE MEYERS
with Larry J. Leech II

NEW YORK

NASHVILLE MELBOURNE

THE GREATEST TRADE

How Losing It All Became Life's Biggest Blessing

© 2017 STEVE MEYERS

Published in New York, New York, by Morgan James Publishing. Morgan James and The Entrepreneurial Publisher are trademarks of Morgan James, LLC. www.MorganJamesPublishing.com

The Morgan James Speakers Group can bring authors to your live event. For more information or to book an event visit The Morgan James Speakers Group at www.TheMorganJamesSpeakersGroup.com.

Shelfie

A **free** eBook edition is available with the purchase of this print book.

CLEARLY PRINT YOUR NAME ABOVE IN UPPER CASE

Instructions to claim your free eBook edition:
1. Download the Shelfie app for Android or iOS
2. Write your name in **UPPER CASE** above
3. Use the Shelfie app to submit a photo
4. Download your eBook to any device

ISBN 978-1-68350-037-7 paperback
ISBN 978-1-68350-038-4 eBook
ISBN 978-1-68350-039-1 hardcover
Library of Congress Control Number:
2016905788

Cover Design by:
Rachel Lopez
www.r2cdesign.com

Interior Design by:
Bonnie Bushman
The Whole Caboodle Graphic Design

In an effort to support local communities, raise awareness and funds, Morgan James Publishing donates a percentage of all book sales for the life of each book to

Habitat for Humanity Peninsula and Greater Williamsburg.

Get involved today! Visit
www.MorganJamesBuilds.com

TABLE OF CONTENTS

ACKNOWLEDGEMENTS

I want to thank my family and friends for putting up with me during some trying times.

Thank you to my father and mother for instilling values that allowed me to overcome adversity.

I want to thank Larry J. Leech II for helping me polish this book and Brad Rhame for helping me get everything down on paper.

Thanks to my sister Madison for helping me with key facts and to friends— Bob, Gary, Jesse, Nancy, and Ron—for reading and providing feedback.

I want to thank my son for providing me with the inspiration to write this book. He loves the Lord and has a beautiful soul. God has plans for him.

I want to thank Morgan James for believing in my story and helping me release it to the world.

I want to thank my Lord and Savior, Jesus Christ, for never giving up on me.

Chapter 1

HOW TO LOSE NEARLY HALF A MILLION DOLLARS IN TEN SECONDS

D o you know what it feels like to lose $480,000 in one day? Better yet, in just ten seconds?

Maybe only a gambler or another trader can understand that feeling, that complete sense of loss. A sudden loss. Not being able to feel your limbs is very real, like your extremities are no longer attached to your body. Putting together a string of words for a coherent thought becomes nearly impossible. The earth beneath your feet falls way until reality sets in and you slam back into terra firma with a thud.

That thud can drive a man to his knees. To either pray or suffer. I agonized in silence. I couldn't tell my Kathryn, my wife of eleven years at the time.

The day before I found out, I'd packed everything Kathryn, our six-year-old son Luke, and I needed into our Cadillac Escalade for a short trip to Atlanta. She needed dental surgery and after months of research settled on a doctor located there. Under the clear blue skies people love in the Sunshine State, we left early from our home in southwest Florida. We weren't super rich like many in the area, but weren't lining up for food stamps either. I drove the first few hours of the nine-hour drive. Somewhere between Sarasota and Tampa, I asked her to take over so I could check on the market. It'd have been easy for me to stay home and manage my accounts from there. This surgery was a big deal to her so I wanted to go for support and help take care of our son. She climbed into the driver's seat and took off. I settled in the passenger seat.

Between Tampa and the Georgia line, Interstate 75 has long stretches of wide open spaces dotted with thousands of billboards. The sometimes monotonous hum of the tires on the road can easily lull a passenger to sleep. With my satellite card and adapter from Radio Shack, I plugged in my computer.

Ten, fifteen years ago, I wouldn't have been able to accompany her on the trip. I would've stayed home, tied to my desk tracking the market on multiple monitors. But, like many occupations nowadays, modern technology has unchained me from my desk and allowed me to roam free.

I roamed right into my market program while my wife barreled toward Atlanta. I let the computer boot up and everything seemed fine. Until I clicked on my actual trade system. A bright red light flashed repeatedly on the screen. My computer made a strange noise like it might lift off from my lap and fly about the automobile. I'd heard stories from friends who watched flames erupt from the vents in their laptops as the hard drive burned up. Worried that I might suffer the same fate, I snatched the adapter from the socket and powered down.

I shoved my laptop back into its case and, thinking the problem was the adapter, figured I'd check on my account the next day. We got to the hotel around dinner time and settled in for the evening. I didn't think about the computer or the market for the rest of the night.

I should have.

The next day she left for her pre-op appointment and I stayed at the hotel to take care of Luke. Between 7:00 and 7:30 a.m., my cell phone rang. Thinking it might be her needing some information for paperwork, I grabbed my phone right away and looked at the caller ID. My handler at the clearinghouse. That's odd, I thought.

"You going to wire in your margins?" he said, a little agitated.

"I shouldn't have a margin call."

"You do." The agitation in his voice was still evident.

"How much is it?"

He told me, but my brain couldn't comprehend what he said. At first, I thought he said $400 dollars. He wouldn't call for that amount. I didn't understand the reason for the call. Like lava inching down the side of a volcano, the information burned into my brain in increments. My mind went from the $400 to $4,000. Still didn't make sense. He wouldn't call for that little either.

Hundred. Thousand. The words tumbled through my mind on spin cycle. The buzzer sounded and the words fell together. Hundred thousand. Four hundred and eighty thousand dollars.

I don't remember ending the call, and I wandered around the room. I felt as if someone had punched me in the stomach. The physical reaction was very real. I went through that once before, during my first commodity loss in my early twenties. I recovered, but at this moment, nearly half a million dollars was gone. Wow. What was I supposed to do? The initial reaction is to panic, but you can't. If you panic, you'll make a mistake you may not recover from.

I turned on my computer and logged into the trading center. I stared at the screen. I had bought 25 contracts of corn until I reached my max of 400. That wasn't the problem. Corn had gone down twenty-five cents. Down. That was the problem. Why couldn't corn have gone up? Or stayed flat?

I need to give him an answer. To wire money I'd have to finagle something around with the banks to hold some stuff. They might have let me go with $100,000 for a day or two. But not this. Not $480,000. They wanted the money now.

Kathryn got back from her appointment and we decided to take a walk around a big mall nearby. The mall could have been across town or on another planet. Despite her surgery, despite being in Atlanta to help take care of Luke, I could only focus on one thing: a plan to make the margin call. She may have wanted to buy something. Facing that kind of loss, I might have balked at buying anything for even ninety-nine cents.

We walked and she talked, but I really didn't hear her. I was on that other planet thinking and strategizing about what I needed to do. I didn't want to sell off. That'd put us in a hole we'd probably never recover from. I pulled myself together the best I could. Fighting off the fight-or-flight feeling, I ran numbers and scenarios in my mind. It's like being somewhere, but not really there—an an out-of-body experience. I'd gotten very good at carrying on a conversation, but over in another part of my brain I'd be thinking about the market. It's really not fair.

At one point, Kathryn looked over at me. "Are you all right?" she said. "Where did you go?"

I couldn't tell her. Not yet. I didn't want to send her into a panic the day before her surgery. I had to come up with something by the end of the day. They wouldn't let me go into the next day. I could have scrounged up the money, if I panicked. I could have liquidated everything, shoveled money around. But then, it's gone. Then you start over in a hole. No one wants to do that. Sometimes starting over is the only choice. Fortunately, it wasn't for me.

I've learned over the years trading is much like being a hitter in baseball. You're only one hit away from a starting a streak. I'd been disciplined over the last few years, trying to slowly build. Then, bam, despite the discipline, it's gone. In ten seconds.

I talked to myself while trying to figure out a plan, going through my options and thinking maybe I can do this or this. While we walked and she talked some more, I came up with a plan to buy me more time. This plan allowed me to margin up. Because I believed the market would bounce back, I figured out how many contracts I wanted to carry forward and then wire in whatever I had at the end of the day. My mood lightened. This was a good plan. A plan that not only could, but would, work.

I called my broker when we returned to the hotel. These guys trusted me so they agreed to give me twenty-four hours, enough time to get through Kathryn's surgery and recovery, but more importantly, for the market to rebound.

I sensed a bounce back in the corn market. And it did. At the end of that day I had to liquidate enough to make the call and to keep my word, which is very important to me.

The next day I was able to settle everything. Thanks to another banner day in the market, my $480,000 loss shrunk to a mere $20,000. I considered that a victory. It's not often a loss of twenty grand feels like a victory. But it did. I could feel my limbs again and the gut punches subsided. Battered and bruised like a championship fighter, we returned to Florida only a little poorer.

That situation took me back to my first commodity loss. That constant feeling of dread and suffocating weight. When a person loses that much money, it's important to keep a cool head, but it's darn near impossible. I kept telling myself that I'd be okay. I knew I would, but in the midst of the crisis, it's tough. Very tough. It's worse than a dark cloud hanging over your head. It's your life. Your hopes. Your dreams.

There is truth to the old adage that cooler heads prevail. I lost more money than most people can fathom because of a computer glitch. When I logged on in the car, my mouse must have been over the "buy" button and, in those ten seconds, bought twenty-five corn contracts faster than I could have done it manually. Today, regulations keep limits in check. If this happened now, I'd probably lose no more than $60,000 at the most. Something much more manageable than $480,000. Rules were lax back then. Another trader didn't have safeguards and he lost $150,000,000. Yes, millions.

I couldn't imagine losing that kind of money. I'm not like some traders who worship money. I don't, but I was obsessed. And that started at a very young age.

Chapter 2
AN EARLY START TO
MY GAMBLING WAYS

B eing a third-generation cattle man, I got to learn from two of the best—
my dad's dad, and, of course, my dad. People have long said the first
generation starts a business and does all it can to get it off the ground.
The second generation works harder, invests their entire life into it, but plays
harder. The third generation comes in and loses everything." I wanted to break
that cycle in my family.

My grandpa started cattle trading when he was a humble grocery
store manager in Ponderosa, Wyoming, in 1952. Although the manager,
he enjoyed working in the butcher department and became an expert on
the various cuts of meat. He became the "go-to" guy for anything special.
Soon he began buying livestock on the side, and that's how our family
business started.

After my dad graduated from high school, he put everything he had into
getting the livestock business going. In Western Wyoming, cattle trading—
if a person can master the art—can be a lucrative business. Early on, my
dad was driven to become something—for a good reason. He wanted to

become bigger and better so his family could be bigger and better. Nothing against his dad, but my dad's determination played right into the family business stereotype.

Despite his hard work, life wasn't always comfortable for my family. When mom and dad got married after she graduated from high school, like most kids, they had nothing. Mom told me once she borrowed money from her father-in-law to buy milk. That may not seem like a big deal, but back then children didn't ask parents for money. Mom swallowed her pride to ask my grandfather for that money. And in a much more embarrassing situation, my parents lived in a rat-infested home for a while.

Dad worked long hard hours, including nights because he had a vision. He worked diligently toward it, and remained faithful to his vision of growing the business and providing a comfortable lifestyle for my mom, sisters, and me. This drove him. Many might say he was obsessed.

Part of this vision was because he went into business with his dad, he wanted the business to remain in the family. So, at an early age, dad started showing me the ropes. By the time I was five years old, I was already running around the corrals, hanging out with the ranchers and doing my chores. There were times we'd have to house the cattle after an auction, but we never kept them for more than a few days. My job description, at that young age, was to make sure they had feed and water. I loved it.

I loved caring for the animals—feeding and watering them. I loved the excitement of being around the farmers and ranchers. More than that, I loved listening to my dad converse with them. And strange as it may seem, I loved the smell. Some wouldn't say that about hay, grass, dust, and horse manure. My dad often said, "That smells like bread and butter."

I soon learned to spot good cattle as I gained an appreciation for the business. On busy weekends, when we had a lot of ranchers bringing their cattle over, a secondary responsibility of mine was to run uptown at noon and bring back a bagful of hamburgers. I remember the ranchers liked me. One gave me the nickname Little Jacky because I was a miniature version of my dad. I liked the nickname. It made me feel like one of the guys. The ranchers joked around a lot, and my dad made sure I felt included in the camaraderie. I was his only son, and it probably wouldn't have been appropriate for my four sisters to be a part of this side of the business.

I spent a lot of time on the road with my dad attending auctions all over the state. We'd get up early and drive for hours. Monday, we drove to Bishop, Wyoming, about 200 miles away. Tuesday, we drove to Monroe, Wyoming, a little over 100 miles. The mid-week jaunt took us to Sanford, Wyoming, a mere seventy-one mile trip. We traveled about 100 miles each Thursday to Fairchance, Wyoming. The week ended with a trip to Tucker, Wyoming, a whopping forty-six miles away.

As you can see, attending auctions was a full-time job, one that allowed me to see more than three thousand cattle cross the corral every five days. I loved the buzz and excitement of each auction. Farmers talked with ranchers, ranchers with buyers, and buyers with farmers. The auctions smelled like home to me, manure, dust and hamburgers.

For a little kid, I found all this exciting. I enjoyed listening to the auctioneer talk faster than any other person I knew. I smiled each time he slammed down his gavel and screamed, "Sold."

By age thirteen I could guesstimate within a few pounds the steaming carcass (gutted and skinned) weight of a walking Black Angus. My dad, of course, could nail it within ounces of course.

We didn't always buy for us. We bought for others if they gave us a specific order. It could be for young calves or slaughter cows. We also bought cattle for the purpose of trading live animals at another auction to capture a profit. People—mostly large companies such as McDonald's—would call my dad and tell him they needed slaughter cattle at a specific price. He'd go to auction, with me in tow, and look for cattle of an appropriate grade, at a better price so he could make some profit. Pretty straightforward. These folks were buying dressed beef—steaming weight on the rail is what we called it. As you can imagine, a large part of the art of cattle trading is accurately guessing that weight. You had to know the moment a cow walked into the corral, just what it would yield in grade and weight. This was my dad's forte. He could tell a good cow the second its tail passed the auction corral's gate. Around fifty-four percent was best—a cow with little fat.

I say it's an art, because not only do you have to be able to instantly spot a good weight on the rail, but there is a tremendous amount of live pressure. In the fall, which is the busy season, an auction could move thousands of cattle a day, often lasting eighteen hours until 3:00 a.m. It was hard work and you had to know your cattle with a near-sixth-sense of accuracy while maintaining your focus.

During the week my dad often slept an hour or so, woke up, and headed to the next auction. Unless I got up early to see him before he left, I'd go days without seeing my dad. This dedication is why my dad succeeded and earned the respect of others in the business.

The business had some other segments as well. We also bought feeder cattle, lighter weight animals that are ready to be fed and eventually slaughtered. My dad looked for feeder cattle weighing between 800 and 900 pounds and to put together a full load. A load is around 50,000 lbs, the capacity of a fully loaded semi-truck. Dad then sent the loads to a feed-lot owned by a friend who lived a couple of hundred miles away in Bishop, Wyoming. This friend fed the cattle around the clock for months until each reached the ideal slaughter weight of 1,300 pounds. Depending on the market price for slaughter steers and heifers, the cattle would make or lose money. You learned to make decisions based on profitability. If you hit a good market, it could be quite lucrative.

We also bought cheap cattle and resold them at various actions in Wyoming, Nebraska, and South Dakota, three of our biggest trading areas. This segment also took a bit of mastery. The key was to get a great price on cattle and then sell these cattle at auction in an area where you knew prices were a little higher. Our contacts alerted us to a trend developing. If the price of that trend was higher than our local area, we could buy and send animals there for profit.

Dad and I found value everywhere. At sale time you may be competing against four or five buyers and they'd fill their loads up, and might not bid on much after. Some guys showed up to bid for one company. When they filled their order, they left. When the competition had filled their orders with cattle left to sell, other buyers could snag some cheap cattle.

Dad and I bought up what we could and then sell these cattle off in the hope of making a profit. Of course, you hope you could get more money out of them in an area where there was more need, but social skills and reputation was the art of this segment. My dad had good relationships with the livestock auctions. Often the auctioneers tried to get the price up a bit for him, if the sale was a little slow. But there would almost always be a hotspot somewhere. If everyone was dumping their cattle in dad's area, he'd buy them, and ship the cattle down south, which to us in Wyoming meant just about everywhere. Mostly we shipped to South Dakota, Nebraska, and Montana. Sometimes we heard from people in Texas if they needed the cattle, but not our services. Dad figured his transport costs quickly, before he bought the cattle. And he was really good at it. So this was true "live" cattle trading. And it wasn't always cattle. If pigs were going at a great price, we'd snatch them up too. It usually worked out really well.

I admired my dad's quick mind. He seemed to sense the coming trend. Even at that young age, I felt I'd never be as good as him. I wanted to be, but he was put on this earth to be a cattle buyer. I wasn't so sure I was.

When it came to business, however, Dad had a "sink or swim" mentality. One time when I was about thirteen, he handed me his cell phone to make a call to a seller. Dad, one of the first people I know to own a cell phone, need a specific cattle. We were on the road to an auction. He dialed a number, gave me the phone, and told me to negotiate with the sellers. I took a deep breath and waited for them to pick up. There was no chance of saying no to my dad. The guy picked up and I proceeded to tell him what buyer I was with and told him what we needed. I negotiated pretty well and made a deal with the seller.

I hated being put on the hot seat. He could have warned me. I felt unsure and insecure. Of course, I loved my dad and didn't want to disappoint him or let him down.

Before we hung up the guy asked to talk to my dad. I put him on the line and my dad asked the guy how old he thought I was. The guy said I sounded about twenty years old. Dad smiled and told him my age. The guy said, "No way." Dad laughed. Of course I could never do a twenty year-old's job. I was completely green but I knew how to talk the talk, and my dad knew that.

Another time, my dad thought it might be good experience for me to buy some slaughter sows. He needed to put a load together to send back East. He took me to the auction and told me to bid on the hogs I thought were good.

Well these hog buyers weren't going to let a thirteen year-old buy anything. I bid on the good hogs, playing the game as I knew how. I made all the right moves, but those guys obviously couldn't stomach being outbid by a kid. I didn't understand that in the heat of the moment and when I didn't win a single bid, I was crushed. The auctioneer came over and shook my hand and thanked me. I looked up a little confused to see my dad with a huge grin on his face. Because of those buyers' pride, I had raised the prices for those hogs astronomically. My dad patted me on the back and said not to worry. He told me they do the same thing to him when he goes to an auction far away and don't know him. He said I did the right thing by raising the prices.

When I was about fifteen, I'd had a good deal of experience at the auctions by now, but was by no means qualified to buy. Bidding against adults still overwhelmed me. Their livelihoods depended on their success and failures. Mine didn't. Being a teenager who'd much rather be goofing off with his buddies, I'd sometimes zone out. At an auction, every buyer is given cards you use to bid with. These helps the auction staff track buys to tally at the end of the event. During one of my daydreaming sessions, my dad gets up and says he's going to the bathroom. He told me to take over and tossed me his cards. I freaked out and told him I couldn't. I had no idea what was going on. He didn't listen and said, "You know what you're doing. Just do it." He left and didn't return for forty-five minutes.

Right away it appeared I was in over my head. I thought I knew slaughter cows but I was getting hammered by the other buyers. I've never been so embarrassed in my life. With each bid, the nasty looks grew more intense. Eventually I tried to rely on the auctioneer who was giving me little hints. That didn't help either.

A man of unwavering excellence, my dad quietly demanded the same from his family. He knew we could do it. Whether we knew it or not. He'd throw us into the fire and sort of say, "You'd better have learned something by now."

Despite my dad's hard work and long hours, he made time for my four sisters and me. All my sisters were cheerleaders, and he rarely missed their games. I can remember the times on one hand that my dad missed a baseball game of mine. And I remember one game he did attend. I built a nice little career hitting singles and doubles. But in this particular game I struck out for the first time.

That bothered me for the rest of the game. Every time I looked at my dad, he was leaning over the fence not saying a word.

In the car after the game, he said, "Good game, huh?"

"It was a bad day," I said, looking up at him a little confused.

"That's okay." He smiled down at me. "I have bad days too."

"You do?" I asked, surprised.

I couldn't imagine a universe where my dad had a bad day. It seemed he was always in control and on top of everything. Dad was a man of excellence, and radiated a sense of control and success in everything he did. His comment really did shock me, but it made me feel better. Made me realize I didn't have to be perfect.

That interaction was one of the few times I can remember we discussed something other than the cattle business. But I loved being with my dad. Some of my best memories are from our hunting trips. He took me on my first trip when I was five. He sometimes traveled to look at farmer's cattle, and if there was time, we'd stop and hunt along the way. Other times we hunt the farm my mom inherited from her parents about thirty miles away from our hometown in Victor, Wyoming. We'd get up at five in the morning, make hardboiled eggs and coffee. Yes, I drank coffee at that age. We'd be sure we arrived before the sun came up, when the deer were on the move. I cherished those days. Just me and Dad doing guy stuff.

We'd talk about the hunting and what was going on at the moment, but mostly we talked about business. We never had any really in-depth personal conversations but at that point, it didn't really matter. I enjoyed any time I could get with my dad.

I was hanging out with my idol.

Chapter 3

GROWING UP IN
A SMALL TOWN

I'd be lying if I said growing up the only boy in a family with four sisters didn't have an impact on my life. My eldest sister Hannah is six-and-half years older than me. Madison is four years older, and Brooke is three years older. I loved my sisters dearly, but all I wanted was a brother. When I was six years old, my mom became pregnant again. I hoped and fervently prayed for a brother. My prayers went unanswered when Lisa was born.

I'll never forget my mom consoling me when my dad took my sisters and me to the hospital to see our newest sibling. I sat on the edge of the bed and was intrigued by my baby sister. But I also expressed my disappointment. "Mom, even the dog is a girl."

Eventually I made peace with having another sister and wrote little notes for my mom. She kept some. One of her favorites says, "Gee Mom, I thought it was a boy but it didn't turn out that way. Oh well, Steve."

Being raised in a small town like Ponderosa, Wyoming, has some huge advantages. For one, sports is a large part of the culture. It seemed everyone was into some kind of sport—football, basketball, baseball, and track and field.

Sports gave my dad and me the opportunity to get close. He was supportive and rarely missed a game. He often told me how proud he was of my success on the field. When the ranchers came over to the house, and they'd be standing looking at the cattle, I'd hear my dad say "Steve is a really great athlete." The farmers nodded and asked more about me. Sometimes he'd go on to sing my undeserved praises. I'd overhear his comments and that pushed me to step up and do something great.

We not only played hard on the field, we learned to play hard off. That usually meant drinking, and later on women. I remember in the fourth grade I snuck my first beer, an Olympia beer, from our downstairs fridge. I cracked it open, chugged it down, and grinned like I was the Fonz. I went upstairs and on the way to my room, I stopped and hugged my mom. She asked me why I smelled like beer. Being a genius ten-year-old, I said our neighbor gave me some. Of course she was up in arms, and immediately grilled the neighbor, who promptly shot down my ruse. But, believe it or not, I never really got into trouble. My act was written off as mischievous kid behavior, which was true, to a certain degree, a common attitude of a small-town culture.

Another time I got away with what could have been a major mistake. By the time we got to high school, things had escalated a bit. My friends and I had earned a bit of a reputation for being willing to push just about any envelope. In 1980—my sophomore year—our baseball team made it to the state tournament being held in a city about seven hours away. Four of us got together and took the Amtrak train to the western side of the state. We spent the entire trip partying. We were supposed to stay with host families but we told the coach we were staying with friends of my parents. Coach, trusting his star players, said, "No problem."

We pooled our money and got a hotel room. Before long we met four girls at one of the games and started hanging out. The girls had a car and were definitely down to party. They drove us around town and pretty soon it ended up kind of like *Animal House*. In fact, our lives were quickly becoming a mirror of the classic movie. With no rules, and no accountability, we were in our element indulging in booze and women. We were already hooked on both. And seldom got caught.

We were athletes and knew we could get away with more stuff than most kids. I was definitely no exception. I remember hanging out with a kid called Logan in the fall of sophomore year at Ponderosa High School. He and I did a lot of crazy stuff together. But nothing serious, just mischievous stuff until one night when we attended a girls' away basketball game. We settled into the packed gym about three-quarters up in the stands. Bored midway through the game, Logan pulled out a firecracker and said, "I dare you to light this and throw it." I wasn't scared to do it, but I wasn't a sucker to take all of the blame either. I said no.

"Whatever, I'm gonna light it and you throw it," he said. Before I could turn him down again, he lit the thing, and handed it to me. Without hesitating I launched it over the crowd. It exploded just behind Ponderosa team's bench. In the tiny gym it sounded like a .50 caliber gunshot. People screamed, the players freaked out, and the referee immediately stopped the game. Everyone was looking around to see who the culprits were. I realized the situation was a lot more serious than I had figured.

Sitting a few rows in front of us was the bus driver, Darnell Hopkins. I'm not sure whether he just liked us or if he just jumped to a conclusion but he pointed to a senior called Bohannan and shouted, "It was that kid. I saw him." Bohannan, so drunk he could barely keep his head up, took the fall. Security took Bohannan away and the game resumed.

That wasn't the end of it. Monday morning we heard about a big investigation into the incident. We were called in to the principal's office and everyone was looking really grim. "After looking into the details, we realized Bohannan couldn't have done it," administrators told us. We sat there trying to look like two innocent lambs. "Rumor has it you boys were involved."

Logan and I looked at each other in feigned horror. I quickly piped up, "I swear I didn't light any firecracker." Logan followed on my heels and said, "I swear I didn't throw any firecracker." Of course, we were telling the truth, but twisting it and this meant absolutely nothing to me. I had become quite good at manipulating the truth. The principal and the head girls basketball coach glared at us. They had no evidence. If they had a shred of proof, we would've been suspended on the spot. We left humbled. Until we got far enough down the hall to cackle like hyenas.

I caught wind a few weeks later the cheerleaders planned to honor Logan and me with a giant firecracker at a pep rally. Although hilarious and would fuel my growing reputation as a prankster, the last thing I needed was to be suspended. Receiving a firecracker would've been an admission of guilt and I knew there'd be repercussions. I called three or four of the lead cheerleaders and begged them not to call us out. After some protest, they disappointingly relented. Needless to say the incident hung over us for a few months, but eventually blew over.

We weren't always fortunate however. About six months later we were all getting spring fever and came up with a plan to bring some alcohol to choir the next day. A handful of the "cool" kids, went to the bathroom for a cocktail before choir started. "Alcohol loosens up the vocal chords," someone said and we laughed. Choir class was held in a separate building just across the street from the high school. If we arrived a little early, we could have about two or three drinks each before we had to be in our seats.

Ted Deetsch, a senior, said he'd bring beer. Others chimed in they'd bring something too. I announced I'd bring something from my parent's bar in our basement. That night I filled a large ginger ale bottle with Canadian Club whiskey and stashed it in my school bag. The seven of us crammed into the bathroom at the appointed time with assorted beverages. We decided to chug a few beers first. But the beer was frozen. Ted left the beer in his car and a spring frost iced our chances to drink them. Undeterred, we went to my whiskey and each took a few swigs. Soon we were ready to go out and sing.

The next day, we got word we were in deep trouble. Alcohol had been found in the garbage can of the bathroom. Ted had stuffed the frozen beer in the trash can and covered it with paper towels. The cans exploded and released a lovely fragrance in the bathroom. As luck would have it, the choir teacher had noticed the beer on Ted's seat when he walked to school the morning before. Ted was called in for questioning and spilled the beans on every single gentleman in the bathroom. We received a two-day suspension for our troubles.

My reward from overly thrilled father was to shovel manure at our stockyards those two days. Looking back, I guess my punishment could have been a lot worse. Although shoveling crap has never ranked high on my list of enjoyable jobs.

This almost-got-caught and minuscule punishment for randy behavior is one of the blessings of living in a small town in the 1980s. Yes, small towns are great in many, many ways. Unless controversy strikes. And it did to our family when Hannah got pregnant after graduation with her boyfriend Rob Newell. We all adored him. He was a phenomenal athlete and one of the most popular guys in school. Us younger kids looked up to him. For good reason. He made time to talk with us and never displayed the arrogance successful seniors so often do.

He adored my sister. When she announced her pregnancy, ripples of whispering permeated throughout the town. Or course, both families were concerned, as could be expected when a young couple experiences the surprise responsibility of a baby. The two families were the types of people that handled the situation in the best way possible, and rallied around them with love and practical solutions.

Initially, I worried about my sister and Rob. My parents weren't happy. Neither were his. It's understandable. Small-town residents can be judgmental.

Despite receiving a full basketball scholarship to Granite Falls (Montana), Rob wanted to marry Hannah. My parents sat them down and discussed options: school, living arrangements, marriage. My parents, and his, encouraged Rob and my sister to attend school. They also agreed to help out the soon-to-be young family. Both families supported decision to get married, a sign each was determined to get through the situation. The silver lining in the unexpected pregnancy is a grandchild.

One afternoon one of the priests from the parish we regularly attended came to the house to discuss the situation and the wedding. At some point during the visit, the priest announced he would require Rob and Hannah to go through six months of counseling before he'd marry them. My parents were shocked.

Given the circumstance, this made no sense to any of us, and on top of that, there was no such official requirement by the church yet. After taking a moment to gather their thoughts, my folks admitted kids don't make the best decisions sometimes. They explained that if there was any possible way, it was important for the Hannah and Rob to be married in the church. The priest then mentioned an abortion as an option.

My folks were stunned. They couldn't believe what they were hearing and glanced at each other, knowing there was really only one remaining option. My dad showed the priest to the door.

This presented a new dilemma. As long as those priests were the heads of the parish, my family would not go near any of their churches. And once my dad had made a decision, only an act of God, cliché as that sounds, change Dad's mind. Instead of switching churches, for reasons unknown to me, we simply stopped going.

Rob and Hannah did get married and went on to live in the married housing complex at college. Hannah gave birth to a boy they named David. A boy. Although I didn't get a baby brother, I got a nephew.

Not going to church caused a slight shift in the family at first. We didn't give up on God by any means. But it did seem strange to me that my parents had so much loyalty to the parish they wouldn't switch churches. We only attended church when one of the priests was away or a guest speaker filled in. Some Sundays we watched a televangelist on TV. So we didn't quit cold turkey, but there was often a long wait between visits from a guest priest.

I don't think the shift affected me too much. When we did attend service, I spent much of my time thinking about which pro game we'd watch after service. Christianity, or what it meant to have a relationship with Christ, was not very high on my priority list at the time.

Chapter 4
MORE MISCHIEF

I t seems people in the Ponderosa area were born with Wildcats maroon and gold blood in us. Whether the teams were good or bad, people turned out in droves to support the team in season.

My friends—Shawn and Justin—and I all lettered on the field, court, and diamond. We all lettered for three years in football, baseball, and basketball. Traditionally, our football team didn't have much success. Not a good feeling for me, the quarterback. However, the basketball team, on which I was a guard, made the state tournament my junior and senior years. I played second base for the baseball team that made the state tournament two years as well.

After home games, and some away games, fans, parents and players met at the VFW club. We'd discuss the game, celebrate if we won or if we lost, and complain about the ref's role in our defeat. Parents loved to show off their players, and players loved to make their parents proud. By our senior year, Shawn, Justin, and I were fixtures at the club, ruling the social scene much the same way we ruled the sports scene. And after the incident with the priests, I lost a great deal of accountability and had little incentive to change anything.

During my junior year, the baseball team played a game about 100 miles away, a common occurrence because of the sparsely populated state. We were in the midst of a bad season, so the partying started before we played. Our coach, just three years older than us, probably should have deterred our party mentally. We reveled in the fact that he didn't. Like the fictitious Bad News Bears, we could play some ball, even when we partied more than we should. Looking back, we probably might have been better off if he'd at least tried to curtail our partying.

I don't remember how well, or poorly, we played. My focus was elsewhere—on the two bat girls for our opponent who wore uniforms that showed off their assets. These girls were gorgeous, brunette with beautiful smiles. I wasn't the only one attracted to them. I think everyone in the conference wanted to date them. Shawn and I decided we would get their attention and stepped up our A-game, oozing our slickest charm. It worked. We ended up dating them during that summer.

After the game, coach drove the bus to a restaurant for a post-game meal. Still in uniform, the girls showed up. Shawn and I endured a lot of ribbing. But we didn't care. Soon after we left, a car come up behind the bus and flashed its lights. The girls. Coach pulled over. The girls bounced out of the car and requested a goodbye kiss from Shawn and me. Coach Calvin looked at us and said, "Hurry up you boneheads." We bounded out of the bus and obliged, to a chorus of friendly ribbing from our teammates. Living like a king never felt so good.

And everybody enabled us. Coach didn't put a stop to any of our shenanigans, nor did the school. Numerous times I overheard my dad say to his friends, "Yeah, Steve really likes the girls." That gave me the green light, in my teenage mind, to keep up with the fun and play time.

Even my family helped my endeavors. My sister Brooke attended college in Glacier, Wyoming, about three and a half hours away. Head East, billed as "The Midwest's Legendary Classic Rock Band," was scheduled to play there in early May. She called and said I could bring any friends I wanted. She'd even buy the tickets.

Bear, of course, was game for a road trip and some partying. Our only problem, which we didn't see as much of a hindrance, was prom was the next day. We figured we could attend the show and be back the next day in plenty of time to get ready for prom. We didn't want to disappoint our dates. Bear and I had planned the double prom date for weeks. We wouldn't let a concert more than 200 miles away mess that up. But it did.

Bear, six-foot-three and more than four hundred pounds, was not an easy guy to forget. He had thick curly hair and loved to flash jewelry, mostly fake. A fan of J.R. Ewing of *Dallas*, Bear loved to live large, his car included. He drove a big Cadillac, like the one Boss Hog drove in *The Dukes of Hazard*.

We took off for Glacier excited about the show and the promise from my sister to show us a preview of college life. Beer and girls. We arrived at my sister's dorm and the beers flowed moments after we walked in. After the liquid hors d'oeuvres, we headed to a college bar called Lucky's. I was instantly hooked. I'd never seen so many cute girls in one place in my life. All were drunk, too, an added bonus. From there, we headed to the concert. I don't know if it was the alcohol or the music, but that was one of the best concerts I have ever attended. We drank, and danced and sang along for a couple of hours. Paradise couldn't offer anything better than this.

When the concert ended, Bear and I were not ready to call it a night. We ended up at a dance club. We stood at the bar when this drunk guy started in on Bear about his jewelry. Bear ignored the first few comments until the guy said the gems were fake. Bear reached over, took off the man's glasses, ran his largest ring across the lens from corner to corner, and returned the glasses to the man's face. "Only diamonds can cut glass."

The guy was so humiliated he sat there and didn't say a word with a huge scratch impairing his vision. I laughed so hard I nearly fell down. That was Bear. To most, he was the most loveable guy with his quick wit and infectious laugh, but you didn't want to cross him.

We eventually stumbled into my sister's dorm at about sunrise. I slept until 2:00 p.m., much later than I should have in order to make it back to Ponderosa in time for prom in four hours. We didn't leave for another hour, which gave us three hours to get home, shower, pick up our dates for one of the biggest days of our lives, and get to prom.

Bear decided to take back roads in the hope we could shave some time off the trip. Cruising along at close to 100 miles per hour in a car that needed shocks, we landed hard in every dip and sent sparks flying. We laughed. What else could we do?

We got back into town at 5:45 p.m., showered, grabbed our dates, and arrived late to prom. It didn't matter, though. We made it in plenty of time to party again that night.

This behavior was common for us, and probably not much different than other high school kids from around the country. I look back and consider it God's grace that none of us were seriously injured. Or killed. But back then, we felt we were invincible and that we owned the world. Well, at least the town and high school—not a good attitude for an eighteen-year-old immature kid.

My senior year, I was elected president of student council. Shawn was voted to vice president. That only added fuel to our invincibility. We took huge advantage of this status and wandered off campus a few times to drive around town and have fun. Nothing malicious or destructive. Just teenage fun.

The only downer I can remember was losing the State Championship basketball game that year. The championships had been our goal since I was in seventh grade and we came close. We lost by three points. To make matters worse, we felt we were victims of some questionable calls at the end of the game. Not because of the players, but because of an unruly crowd. Don't get me wrong, the athletes could gladly contribute their share of mayhem, but the crowd was getting pretty upset. After the other team's star player was called for a dirty foul, some spectators threw batteries on to the court while they booed. Soon, a few radios were tossed onto the hardwood. I think the refs got intimidated. I'm not bitter. The other team was good. They earned their spot in the title game, just like we did.

We did our best to get over the loss. And the best way was to party and party some more. Near graduation, Shawn, Justin, Bear and I were out cruising. On a school night like this one, we'd load up the car with beer and hope to meet friends or better yet, some girls. We had polished off a a few beers and around 1:00 a.m. we were hungry.

I had the drunken epiphany that we should go up to the school and cook breakfast in the Home Economics room. We found an open boiler room window. We reasoned we technically didn't break in. Justin crawled through and unlocked the door for the rest of us. In the Home Ec room, we found bacon and eggs in the refrigerator. I was elected cook.

The only challenge was not being able to turn on the lights. Instead, my comrades in crime flashed the lights on and off so I could see to cook. Drunk and trying to cook in what amounted to a strobe light, I turned up the heat too high. Soon smoke poured off the pan with the bacon, which now was burnt to a crisp. Before I cracked all the eggs into the pan, the grease from the bacon burned off, filling the room with black smoke.

Laughing, we opened the windows. When the smoke cleared enough, we ate the overcooked bacon and rubbery eggs. We dined, in our minds anyway, like gentlemen at a fine eating establishment. Not surprisingly, no one wanted to clean the dishes. We decided to just scrape the plates and put them back in the cupboard.

The next morning, Shawn and I walked were headed to home room when we passed Mrs. Steele, the Home Ec teacher, standing in her customary spot. I whispered to Shawn, "Act cool."

"How was breakfast last night, boys?" she asked with a smile.

We tried to act baffled. Nothing else was said until Shawn ran into her fifteen years after graduation. He asked how she knew. She replied, "Who else would it have been?"

She had a point. No one else. Just us. We thought back then that no one knew anything, but they knew everything. Ponderosa is not a sprawling metropolis. It's a small town where residents pretty much knew about everyone else's business.

We lived like kings, and were having the time of our lives. We developed attitudes to match, not a good thing for an immature eighteen-year-old. We weren't malicious, but some of the aspects of our lifestyle—especially the way we treated women—were wrong. I think we knew it but didn't change because on the surface we didn't care. We believed we had time to change later. Thankfully, we all did.

But not until we endured a few more hardships. I know I did. When a person lives like a king, at least in their mind, it's inevitable you meet the one woman who can truly wreck your life.

Chapter 5
GIRLS, GIRLS, GIRLS

My buddies and I saw girls as a challenge, never really as individuals. I don't recall anyone having a talk with me about how to treat women or how to respect them. I was exposed to girls at a really young age and became hooked. I'm sure I didn't mean any harm back then, but now I greatly regret the decisions I made. Nothing was intentionally malicious. I think most of the stuff my friends and I got up to was just out of boredom.

Before I left Ponderosa, my neighbor and science teacher, William Osteen, lectured us boys about a key aspect of college life. "Now boys I just wanna warn you now. When you get up to school there will be a lot of women looking for their MRS degree. You need to watch out for them."

"What do you mean?" I asked, wondering if this was some weird major.

"They're looking for a husband," he said.

I got it. That scared the living heck out of me.

My dad was happy for me when I was accepted into college. He pulled me aside one day and said, "Son, I want you to go to college and have a great time, because I wasn't able to go."

His words seemed a blessing to enjoy my college experience, which I very well intended to do. I was determined to make the most of my secondary education. By make the most of it, I meant party for as long as I possibly could. After college, I knew I was doomed to a sealed fate in the family business. I know it sounds downright awful, but when the family business is your only option, coming to grips with that takes some time.

My dad only asked one thing of me in regards to college: keep Fridays open. He needed me to travel to auctions for him. I didn't mind for the most part, I had potential to make more money on that one day than my friends who worked minimum wage for four or five days a week.

I stayed in the dorms for the fall quarter 1982 and winter quarter 1983 for one reason—to meet other kids. Shawn's room was just down the hallway. He had another kid staying with him, but our two doors were open the entire time. We'd just treat the hallway like it was an adjoining space, going back and forth to each other's rooms all the time. Bear started college in spring quarter 1983 and we moved out into an apartment together. With the drinking age nineteen in Glacier, you can imagine the mayhem. Our partying went from wild to pandemonium.

My playground for girls expanded when I went to college. The girls in Ponderosa were great. The girls at the University of Wyoming, Glacier, were better. I didn't wait long to date someone, maybe a few weeks, certainly less than a month. And sure enough, Osteen's words came true. During a boys' night out, we ended up at the dance club that Bear and I went to after the Head East concert. Instead of tables, this place created small private sections with smoky colored plastic dividers. Customers sat on rounded couches. My buddies and I were having a good time when the bouncer came over and pointed at me. The girl I'd been seeing for about three months wanted to see me in the parking lot. She wasn't old enough to enter the club. While we worked on a scheme to get her inside, she said in a serious tone, "I have to ask you something."

I paused for a second, not sure where this was going. "Sure, go ahead."

"Do you think we'll be married this time next year?"

I couldn't respond. So I drove her to the dorms. Because I hadn't said a one word since her question, she was pretty upset. Finally, I said, "Sorry, this is not happening." At the tender age of nineteen, it was the only way I knew to deal with a girl chasing her Mrs. degree. She got out of the car. I never saw her again.

After dodging that bullet, spring quarter '83 ended up being the most fun of my college career. I took a super-light credit load, allowing me to devote my time to partying. Shawn and I quickly landed new girlfriends. This time our girlfriends were into having fun, like us. With Bear as a roommate, the partying was pretty much nonstop. My girl Emily could hang, but Shawn's couldn't and he dumped her after three months. Emily was laid back. We didn't get on each other's nerves, so on a whim I took her home to meet my parents.

My parents were naturally hospitable people, but my nerves were still on edge. Who isn't when they take someone home to their parents for the first time? Friends at school loved Emily because of her quick-witted humor and engaging personality. I felt Mom and Dad might like her, and they did. We laughed a lot that weekend. It seemed Emily had been part of the family for a long time.

With my feelings for her growing, I took Emily home again a few weeks later. This time my parents weren't cordial. Worse, they didn't hide it. I got mad, but kept the peace during the weekend. Even if they didn't approve of her for some reason, I was old enough to make up my own mind.

During summer vacation a few Fridays later, I was back in Ponderosa after a day's work. I had plans to meet Emily the next day at the lake, about an hour from our respective home towns. She said she'd call and let me know for sure. But I never heard from her. I was pretty mad she had just blown me off. I called sometime during the weekend to let her know I was pretty ticked off. She told me she had called and left a message with my mom.

I stormed into the kitchen and confronted my mom. "I am old enough to make up my mind, okay?" I said in a tone louder than what I normally used when speaking to my mother. "Don't you ever withhold a message from me again."

I heard Dad stomp from the living room. He barreled into the kitchen and put his finger in my face. "Boy, don't you ever talk to your mother like that again."

I was still pretty fired up, and feeling like a big, college man, I challenged him, "What are you gonna do about it?"

My dad sized me up and for a second, I thought he might just snap my neck right there. I was not about to back down. He shook his head slightly and said, "You know what, you're really starting to piss me off."

"So get pissed off," I chirped, but I knew it was time to bow out. If it got any more heated, something bad was sure to happen. So I turned my back on my dad and left. After I exited, my body quivered for a while. I'd never had a showdown like this with my dad.

I drove to Emily's parents' home town and stayed with her for three days. I didn't talk to my parents the entire week. With work coming up on Friday, I couldn't put off talking with them much longer. I wasn't about to blow up my entire future over a fight about a girl. On Thursday night I called my dad and asked some trivial question about work the next day. I added "So about last week... I just had to blow off some steam."

Dad said, "Sometimes you have to do that." Nothing more needed to be said, nor was it.

The following summer, in 1984, Emily decided to attend University of Wyoming in Laramie, about two hours away. Neither of us figured our relationship would last. We tried, seeing each other a few times. When we broke up, I know my parents were relieved.

After a while, the excitement of the party scene wore off. By the time I was a junior in 1985, I was honestly getting pretty sick of it. One day while I walked to class, I passed a friend of mine, who was walking with two girls, one of whom was with him. I gave the other girl a second look because I hadn't seen her at school before. My friend stopped. After a quick greeting, he said, "This is Tammy."

It was obvious the girl had asked who I was. I found out Tammy intended to be at school only for a short time because she had a little girl and was recently divorced. I figured I'd ask her out because she isn't likely to be into the party scene, and I could just stay home and watch a movie with her when I needed a break.

I was wrong. Tammy liked to party. A lot. Her intention was to attend school for one quarter and have as much fun as possible. Great. No long-term commitment. No strings.

Instead of looking at the situation and thinking, "Her daughter is away from her, what kind of mother could do that?" I had just found my second wind to keep partying. Tammy and I partied like proverbial rock stars the entire quarter. I enjoyed her company. And she had a way of making me feel really good. She was honestly more of a buddy, which was pretty new to me in a girlfriend. She was usually agreeable to do whatever I wanted, even go to football games with me. She also seemed to cherish our time together. It seemed I was important in her life, something else new for me.

When the quarter ended, so did my fun with Tammy. I was okay with that. I had started the relationship with an end in mind. She went off to airline school. I moved on to other girls and went about my merry business of trying to finish my college degree. After a few weeks, Tammy started calling me again. I figured there was no harm in talking. She'd eventually meet someone while she was at school and I sure didn't keep it a secret I was dating other girls. We talked on the phone for a few months. Then she dropped a bomb. She said she was coming back to Glacier—for me. No one had ever done anything remotely close to that. I did feel flattered.

I couldn't believe she'd come back just for me. If the relationship didn't last, I figured we'd go on with our lives. I didn't ask her to come back for me. She opted to, and she had to understand that, right? What was there to lose?

In the spring 1986, Tammy moved back to Glacier and this time, she brought her little girl with her. They moved in with a friend of hers. As soon as I met her daughter, Tabitha, I was instantly and surprisingly smitten. Tabitha was an adorably smart, cute three-year-old. I quickly fell back into the relationship, hanging out with Tammy and now Tabitha.

Tammy seemed to be getting her life on track too, and our relationship felt sort of "adult" in a way. She landed a good job at a travel agency. The friend Tammy lived with also had a little girl. This gave us an automatic sitter when Tammy and I wanted to go out alone.

I really liked Tammy but bad things began to happen. Insecurities, jealousy, and territorial issues surfaced. I dealt with it at first by limiting my interaction with other girls while she was around.

When my friends told me they weren't too fond of her, I got a little annoyed with them. It was my relationship, and I liked aspects of it—being an adult and getting a glimpse of what it was like to be a dad. One day a friend from Tammy's hometown pulled me aside. "Please be careful with what you're doing. You and Tammy, how do I say this, you come from two different sides of the tracks. Just be careful buddy."

That ticked me off. I knew Tammy. Who was he to warn me? I knew her issues. I decided nobody would tell me what to do. In fact, from that moment on, I became determined in my mission to change her.

For the next semester, Tammy left her daughter back home. I didn't understand the decision, but I wasn't in a place to say anything. I loved Tabitha. She had so much potential. I felt I could really have a profound, positive influence on her if I tried. Tammy came from and broken home and I didn't want Tabitha to.

I knew of only two ways to solve that problem. First, because we could obviously only do family-friendly stuff, but I'd make sure Tabitha was included in our activities. Second, I'd take them both home to meet my parents.

Chapter 6

TOUGH LESSONS

I took Tammy and Tabitha home often. Tabitha really was an adorable little girl. I loved her as if she was my biological daughter. My parents seemed to love her, too, an instant grandchild. Tammy, on the other hand, was treated better by my parents than Emily, cordial at least. But I sensed they didn't trust her. Like most parents, they saw the "real" Tammy, even when I couldn't. Which made going the extra mile for Tammy baffling to me.

During my Spring quarter, April 1986, problems with Tammy exploded from nuances to full-blown battles. I had less tolerance for her behavior after dealing with her jealousy and drunken temper for months. I still cared for her, maybe because of Tabitha. Tammy's mean streak also became corrosive. The number of fights and intensity of those battles grew steadily and exponentially. After a while, I wondered why I even bothered.

While I dated Tammy, I still spent every Friday at auction. One time, when I was about to leave for an auction, I received a call from my dad. Something didn't seem right. He said he needed me to do something for him. He said was he was "in a little jam."

"I want you to and introduce yourself to my futures broker, Bill Black. He has an office at the Glacier auction," Dad said. "There is something going on with my trading account. Find out if anything can be done."

Dad's jam surprised me. He handled every aspect of his business impeccably. To hear he was having issues rattled me a little. Dad had never asked for my help before. I felt good that he trusted me, but on the other hand, his request shook me up a little. Well, more than a little. I saw him in a different light now. He became fallible, less than invincible. When your hero becomes human, it takes a little time to get your mind around your new view of them. I wondered, too, why he didn't just call his broker himself. Or make the trip up to see him.

I knew absolutely zip about futures. I'd heard horror stories. The whole thing was a little disconcerting. After thinking about it for a while, I chalked it up to my dad's confidence in me after watching my success in our livestock business. He'd groomed me in that arena and we worked well together.

I drove about twenty minutes from my apartment to this guy's place. I loved the location, ingenious to have the office in an auction barn. I entered the building and was greeted by the ever-present odors of animal manure and dust, which surprisingly never overwhelmed the hamburger smells from the kitchen. I easily found the office of Bill Black Commodities through the set of modest, but classy French doors that separated his spot from the rest of the complex.

Inside the front door sat a desk with a rather serious looking gentleman sitting in a leather chair. He wore slacks and a white dress shirt. He seemed in his late fifties or early sixties with snow white hair. He wore coke-bottle-thick glasses. I thought how sad this guy must be. Then he spoke. In a commanding voice.

After introductions, he pointed to a chair. I sat. While he talked, he pointed to a huge, mechanical quote board that covered three quarters of one wall. Quite the spectacle for someone who had never seen a board before. Numbers flipped over like in old railway stations and airports before the digital age. This board carried all the daily prices and quotes of the livestock at auction.

"So what's going on with our account?" I asked.

"Well, the government has announced a program," he began tentatively. "Right now, there is a glut of milk on the market which appears to be negatively impacting the dairy farmers. Supply and demand you know?"

I nodded.

"The government has decided to give the option to some dairy farmers to sell their herds and offer them a set price to avoid thousands of bankruptcies."

I didn't say anything. I knew from an economics standpoint this didn't sound good.

Bill continued spoon-feeding me the information. "So you have a government dairy buyout which is expected to reduce the amount of milk on the market. As a result, raise the price of milk back to sustainable levels."

Because of the glut of milk, the government stepped in to help out the dairy farmers by buying some cows. The slaughter reduced the milk supply and increased the amount of meat on the market. Retail price for milk at that time was around $2.20 a gallon.

"Is my dad trading dairy futures?" I asked, in surprise.

"Oh no. The fallout of the dairy buyout is the cattle—even though they're inferior quality beef—are sent to slaughter."

"Won't that create a glut of meat on the market?"

"Son," Bill said with a smile, "within minutes of your education in futures, you are indeed more astute than our esteemed government."

I returned the smile. Although I had grasped the information, I didn't understand all of it. It didn't seem right the world worked like that.

"So what has happened is as soon as the government announced the program, it had an immediate impact on the market. Cattle futures have taken a huge hit simply because of how much meat is going to be on the market in the future. The supply will far exceed the demand, which makes the meat less valuable." Bill gave me a pitiful look.

Bill explained the government announced the program in December 1985. Since the announcement, the beef markets had been slowly going down. Those in the inner circle had already started selling. Apparently, my dad wasn't in the inner circle and this was about to bite him in a way that I couldn't fathom at the moment. I didn't like that some had this information before others and used it to their advantage.

"That's the nature of the beast I'm afraid. We would have too." Bill shrugged. "If we knew."

"So what does my dad's account look like?" I asked, still seething a little.

"Your dad went long on his contracts. As a result, and I hate to say it, but he's in quite a position."

"Went long?" I was uncomfortable at how little I knew about all of this.

Bill cleared his throat, apparently thinking for a moment how to best explain. "Futures trading is similar to stock trading, like on Wall Street, except you're trading strictly in agricultural futures.

"The way it works is if you buy a contract, you," he made quote marks in the air, "'go long.' If you sell a contract, that's called 'going short.' You do that when you think the market is going to decline. You'll sell a contract because you're required to buy it back later. You'll buy it back cheaper, thus making profit. It's the only place you can legally sell something you don't own." Bill winked. I smiled and nodded for him to carry on. "Your first transaction is to sell something—a load of cattle—with a promise to buy it back later. Of course you have to know your cattle, which your dad really does.

"Run that by me again" I wanted to make sure I thoroughly understood it.

He did, and this time the idea made a little more sense. I still felt overwhelmed.

"Does being so close to the live cattle affect your judgment?" I had a hunch it did.

"Indeed, it does. Most traders who are involved in the livestock business fight the impulse to be too bullish, no pun intended."

"Because they are so familiar with the actual business of trading, and projecting what cattle will be available months down the road, they are tempted to believe they have inside knowledge?" I clarified, really just thinking aloud rather than asking a question.

"Yes," Bill confirmed. "Many cattlemen, your dad included, are even tempted to get Texas hedged. In fact, this is how many of your dad's positions currently stand, if I am not mistaken."

"Texas hedged?" This was a twist. I felt another stab of anxiety.

"Texas hedged is when you own the live cattle *and* you've also bought the contracts on those loads." Bill arched his brow. "If a trader is so confident the market is going up, he buys the contracts on the physical loads of his cattle, as well as obviously owning the cattle.

"You're not reducing your risk, you're doubling your risk." Bill paused to let the comment sink in. "Your dad was so sure the markets were going higher—and outside of this dairy buyout, he was probably right—he went 'long on the board' too. That means he stands to lose money, not only when he gets a lower price for his loads of live cattle, but also on the contracts he bet on those same loads."

"Is that even legal?" I felt sick.

"Oh it's very legal. And a great way to make money, outside of mishaps."

"Yeah, and a great way to lose money," I said, halfway to myself. Bill gave me a sympathetic look. "So this dairy buyout has just swept his feet out from under him?"

"Precisely," He nodded with another pitiful look. "In all fairness, something of this magnitude hasn't happened in all my years of trading."

Not what I needed to hear to console me. Looking back, my dad was more stressed than he let on. So was the family business. "How much money are we talking about here?"

Bill grabbed my dad's file off a pile to his right and flipped through it. "Worst case, he'd lose just over $78,000 if this tanks completely."

"Oh, brother." A huge loss. "So what can we do?"

"Well you have several options," he said. "You can put a stop in. That's basically an order which says if the price goes below this point, we automatically liquidate our positions, I mean our contracts." He looked at me to make sure I understood what he was about to say. "You're cutting your losses at that point."

"And the other options?" I tried to sound confident, but my inexperience with this didn't provide much.

"You can wait and buy back in, if and when the market stabilizes."

"Which isn't likely because of the dairy buyout." These weren't really options, and I could feel the anger bubbling just under the surface. Dad needed a better way to get out of this mess.

"Or you can reverse the position." Bill wasn't pulling any punches with me. For that, I was thankful. He folded his hands on top of the file.

"I don't understand." I rubbed my face.

In his richest, official tone, Bill said, "It is my opinion the market is going to drop much lower because of this dairy buyout." He paused and I nodded. "When you reverse your position, you realize your losses on the previous trades. You settle up your account. Take it on the chin. Instead of going long, you go short."

"Going short is selling loads right?"

"Contracts. Yes. Basically a contract for a load."

"But what if he doesn't have any loads to sell?" I asked.

Bill explained that if Dad didn't have loads to sell, he could buy contracts putting down only 3 % of the value of the contract. He went on to explain a person doesn't need to know anything about the actual business of livestock to trade futures, although it helps.

An average load is about forty thousand pounds. I did the math quick. Three-percent came out to six hundred dollars. This sounded too good to be true. And it was. A person needed cash to realize their account. If they didn't have it, that caused big trouble.

We took a break during which we talked about the weather, college, and baseball. Anything but livestock and futures.

When he resumed, Bill offered this was the opposite of getting Texas-hedged, "Let's assume, for example, you own a load of fat cattle. It's a forty-thousand pound contract which, as you know, is a truckload of live cattle."

"Truckloads are closer to fifty thousand pounds."

"You're exactly right," he said. "But on paper, fat cattle—as opposed to feeder cattle—actually trade at forty-thousand pounds. Weird, I know, but true."

After I shrugged, he continued, "Let's say you owned two loads of fat cattle and you want to hedge them. You own the cash value of the load, so you're 'long' the cash. If you own two loads, you're going to sell two contracts now, in the spring *if* you believe the market will go up. This way, you're going to lock in your profit now. That is proper hedging, because you own the load, but you're selling the contract against your own load at a decent price right now. It protects you from severe risk and simply locks in your profit."

His simple explanation made sense. I realized my dad had doubled down by betting the loads he owned would increase in price. But the dairy buyout had caused them to drop in price. Insanely.

"So you think we need to reverse and go short on some contracts?" I asked. I was getting the lingo down now, and feeling a little more confident.

"With the steady drop in the market, and the accounts current positions, I think it might be advisable."

If I was able to grasp this concept, why hadn't Bill advised my dad to do this? Why hadn't my dad to come up with the idea? Maybe his stress level was more than he could handle? Or maybe he didn't have time to deal with this issue. He did have a lot of other business dealings to handle.

After a moment of thinking about the options, I said, "Let me talk to my dad and watch these markets for a little while. When the time is right we'll reverse the position."

"I believe reversing is the right choice," Bill said and shook my hand. "Don't wait too long though."

I appreciated the respect—something a young man new to the game needed.

Chapter 7

LEARNING
THE HARD WAY

I didn't really question anything Bill Black told me. My dad trusted him, so I trusted him. I knew nothing about futures, but it did make sense to me. Trading seemed pretty easy actually. One just needed to learn the feel of the market.

I called Dad and explained what Bill said and why. Dad said, "Well keep me posted, if that's what he thinks." End of discussion. He had complete trust in me, his twenty-two-year-old futures trader with one day of experience.

At first, the markets intrigued me and how they related to the actual cattle trade in a detached but powerful way. It seemed the paper-based futures markets wielded more power than the trade of tangible livestock. The appeal of putting hundreds of thousands of miles on a car each year, sweating at auction arenas, and coming home dusty, dirty and tired, was gone. In its place appeared a vision of a grandiose life, filled with excitement, easy money, and all the accompanying trappings.

I knew I had to learn more and I planned to spend the summer studying the craft of trading. Summer classes took a backseat, as did my relationship with

Tammy. Trading and learning about trading became my escape. I visited Bill's office every few days to monitor the market and learn what I could.

While I kept my eye on the market, Bill believed we should reverse our position. The Chernobyl nuclear disaster in April spiked futures prices because of the potential demand for North American beef in Europe. Happiness knocked on my door.

Then left. After the panic of fallout from the Chernobyl accident subsided, the market slid when several newspapers reported the radiation cloud had a much lower impact on Europe than feared. European beef and grain were barely tainted, if at all. I naively blew this off and believed more demand was on its way.

Instead, concern swung back to the approaching glut of dairy meat. Prices dropped and by the end of May the cattle market was nearing an all-time low. I received an unexpected call from my dad. He sounded stressed. "I need you to go into Bill's office and see what we can do to hold this thing together."

I went to the office and asked Bill, "What do you think?" I knew the June cattle were trading at an unbelievably low fifty-three cents.

"Some traders believe we could go as low as forty-six," he said. "That'd double your current losses from here." He didn't have to do the math for me, I was already feeling sick. "We could take the option of reversing the position and make up the losses on the way down."

Bill recommended reversing the positions looking to make up our losses on a drop to forty six cents. If the market started to go up instead of down, we would do our best to limit those losses. I agreed, without hesitation.

When I stepped in, Dad had thirty-seven contracts open. I reversed position with my first trade. At the end of May, we sold those Texas-hedged contracts at a pretty big loss, but since the market was likely going down to forty-six, we could make the money back by opening new contracts, and selling short. Selling short was selling something you don't own with the promise to buy it back later. Instead of buying low and selling high, we'd be selling high, and hopefully, buying back low.

The market dropped, like Bill thought. Yes, we took a big hit, but not as much if we didn't reverse. The market bounced back and with it, my blood pressure. Then we had to get out and suffer another loss. It was bad enough taking the first hit, now I reversed at the wrong time and suffered another blow. I now sat with no positions and no plan. Doubt crept in.

My first month of trading seemed like a lifetime. Learning on the fly about reverse positions, adding positions to make up losses quicker, day trading—all this overwhelmed me. I went into Bill's office and he handed me June's trading report. There are two aspects—both simple—to reading your month's numbers. The open trade gain or loss was purely on paper. "Open" accounts were still active, and could go one way or another until the contracts were closed—sold or bought back. This number reflects your current position at the close of the month on open accounts. A realized gain or loss is the profit or losses you've taken because you've either willingly closed contracts or had to close them because of the time span of the contract.

We closed 370 contracts. In contrast, my dad closed no more than twenty contracts since the beginning of the year. The staggering number of contracts reflected how many day trades I made and the number of positions I reversed, twice. All this work should have produced a profit. It didn't. After my first month of trading, the realized loss totaled $159,651. In addition, I deposited $28,000 into our account to stay afloat.

Not a good way to start one's trading career.

While spending a lot of time at Bill Black's office, I became friends with Fred Willoughby, a fun guy who put a positive spin on just about everything. I usually saw him slouched over his desk analyzing charts. He taught me the intricacies of the trading ropes as much as he could without stepping on Bill's toes.

In early July, Bill thought we should add hog contracts as well. His livestock analyst called a good hog market so far. If Bill liked the idea, I was all ears. I traded hogs and immediately made a little bit of money while keeping up the cattle trades as well.

Around this time Fred showed me how to forecast using past trends. This was a more "meat on the bones" analysis, if you will. He also got me into cattle options.

"Options are kinda like insurance," he said. "You can't lose more than your policy. Look, cattle options give you the right to be long or short at a specified price. Basically the money you put up is called the premium and that's all you can lose. If you go long and the market drops below your premium, you just lose your premium."

To a lay trader, it still sounds like gambling. But to a kid facing market swings this meant I could lose twice what I'd invested in a contract, options sounded like a sure thing.

"Word on the street is the report is going to be extremely bullish." Fred blinked

I bought a hundred options for around $25,000. We waited anxiously for the cattle on feed report to release Friday at 1:00 p.m. We were so eager to read, Fred and I almost ripped the pages.

The report was extremely bullish, just as Fred called it. The market was expected to open limit up on Monday—at the high point and was expected to go up from there. I had one hour to turn these options into contracts. My hundred contracts would be worth $60,000 on Monday morning. The good news didn't stop there. The report said we might see two or three limit moves over the next week. If that happened, I stood to make $180,000 on these options.

Finally, something in my favor.

The contracts didn't limit up. Instead they traded. I didn't understand the gravity. Instead of making nearly $200,000, I watched my profits dwindle from a real $60,000 on Monday morning to $50,000 to $40,000 and by Tuesday afternoon $30,000.

I leaned over Fred's desk. "What are we going to do? This market is not going to limit up again."

He looked up at the board and nodded. "I think you're right."

"I'm going to bail while I can. I'm still up about thirty K, and I'd like to keep some of it."

"I'm with you man," he said.

By the time I sold the contracts, my profits were down to $20,000. I sighed, and walked into Bill's office to discuss my other contracts. The picture was even bleaker. I was all over the place with more than 200 contracts. The losses were heavy.

"What do you think?" I said to Bill. "These hog contracts seem to be killing me."

"You're all over the place because you're messing with options and things now. I didn't give you that advice."

I was a little taken aback by Bill's tone. "I made a little money on those. How is that affecting me negatively?"

He took off his glasses, cleaned them on his shirt, and shook his head. Instead of addressing me, Bill called Fred outside for a talk. Bill's tone indicated he was not happy with Fred mentoring me. I thought I heard Bill say something about "stepping on his toes." When they returned, Bill said, "Let's take a look at the file together." He sat next to me and we took a big picture look at the trades. We had worked our way back into a fairly large, long position. Since I had reversed twice the market kept going up.

The morning of July 31, Bill pulled me aside when I first walked in. The look on his face terrified me.

"Your account has been on a five-day margin call," he said.

"What?" Why hadn't he told me sooner?

"You're going to be completely liquidated tomorrow," he said, his head shaking a little.

"How much? I'll write a check."

"You can't write a check." His eyes widened. "It has to be a wire."

"Why?"

"Your margin call is two hundred and twenty thousand dollars."

I didn't move. I couldn't. I simply stared at the man I thought was my mentor.

"They're going to liquidate tomorrow, on the sixth day. You need the money today." I think Bill was being nice, but I also sensed he was freaked out a little too.

I left and went home. I fell onto my knees and prayed. Something I hadn't done in a while. "Please God please. I beg you. Help me out of this mess. God, I have lost everything." Then I rambled. "My dad is gonna kill me. Heavenly Father, if you get me out of this mess, I will change. I promise. I will quit drinking and womanizing. I'll go to church regularly. God, just help me get this money back. I am begging you."

I prayed until my knees hurt and moved to the edge of the bed. I needed time to gather up the courage to call my dad. He could hear the nervousness in my voice when I greeted him.

"Are you okay?"

"We've run into a bit of a problem with the trading account."

He was silent for a second. "Yeah? What sort of problem?"

"Basically what has happened is as we've been trading, the market went crazy, and we've taken some losses. The money that was in the account when I took over isn't there anymore. So we don't have enough money to hold on to the contracts we have open unless we wire some money into the account."

"You can't write a check?"

"They need a wire," I paused, needing a moment to gather more courage, "and they need it today. We've been on margin call for five days."

"How much do you need?" He sounded concerned.

"Two hundred and twenty K," I whispered. He didn't say anything, and in a moment of sudden confidence, I blurted, "Please trust me on this. I swear to you we won't lose this. I've been making some profits recently."

I heard Mom in the background asking what was wrong. He muffled the phone, talked with her for a minute, and came back on the line. In the background, Mom begged him, "Jack, don't do this. Please do not do this. We'll lose the house."

"Are you sure we can come back from this?"

"Trust me. We'll come back."

"Just make it happen." He hung up.

I groaned and laid back on the bed. After a few minutes in a catatonic state, I headed back to Bill's office. After taking care of the wire, I read over the month's reports. In July, we closed 272 additional contracts, and eighty new contracts remained open. Among those contracts were 112 hog contracts with a realized loss of $37,000. Through the month, four payments had been made into the account totaling $28,000 in the form of checks.

A total of $220,000 had been paid into the account via a secure wire. I exhaled deeply, bowed my head, and prayed again, "God, I'll do anything for you if you can make this account turn positive. I promise I'll clean up my act."

I later learned God doesn't work that way.

Chapter 8

FROM BAD TO WORSE

After a horrific July of one decision after another, August rolled in and ignited new hopes about making up our $200,000 loss. Nothing like taking a $78,000 debt and nearly tripling it in less than three months. When Dad wired the $200,000 into the account, the market went completely sideways, or what traders call choppy. This continued for the first couple of weeks.

In a sideways market, prices fluctuate little and a trader has little opportunity to make money. There are no trends, except for a typical swing up or down after the choppiness. Smart traders can anticipate which way the market will swing, and at the right moment, go big in that direction. For the time being however, Bill said we should just remain in a holding pattern.

Bill wanted me to hold tight because, and I didn't know it at the time, he was concerned about my account. My margin requirement had grown to almost $300,000 on 200 contracts and some hog contracts as well. This got his attention, and I think he was worried about his liability. He caught me in a good mood one day in his office. "I have a good idea, if you're interested," he said.

Thinking his idea involved trading, I agreed. Bill outlined an idea for me to visit his friend Jacob Sarno in Palm Beach, Florida, for a week. Jacob was a jovial little man and sort of reminded me of a cartoon character. He lived in a condo—large, on the water with a beautiful view and gorgeous furnishings. After dinner with Jacob and his wife, he wanted to chat in private. We went to his office.

"So Bill tells me you are playing with a lot of cars," he said.

"Cars?" I'd never heard that term before in regards to trading.

"Contracts," he said, laughing.

"Well I don't know, I guess sometimes."

"Bill also tells me you don't listen to him and he can never get you to take profits," he added, a little more serious now.

I couldn't believe he just said that. I listened to Bill's advice. I had to. I didn't know what I was doing. I was just trying to learn.

I told Jacob my side of the story because it seemed Bill had only told his side of it.

"I can tell you're a good young man," Jacob said, in an effort to calm me. "We can't undo what has happened. However, I can show you a few things that will hopefully help you."

Still angry, I nodded.

After breakfast the next morning, we took his scooter to his office, a place as beautiful as his home. Jacob employed five people, one a kid, Jim, about my age. Jacob also had a full-time technician who did nothing but charts. Compared to what I had seen, this was a gigantic step up. Jacob ran what was known as a floor trader's system where he'd buy and sell contracts all day long for a small move. His goal was to make $100 per contract, known as scalping a market. At the end of a day, he'd have traded more than a hundred contracts. Doing this prevented him for the giant exposure of carrying too many contracts at one time. He shared that only a few times a year a trader should load up. "Interestingly" he said, "We are approaching one of those times."

I learned a lot from Jacob and the week with him was the highlight of my year. For one, Jacob called certain packers in the industry for the status on meat sales to retailers. This took the guesswork out of the trading. Second,

Jacob made a lot of money with his system. Serious money, like in the amounts I couldn't begin to get my mind around. At the time, I couldn't emulate his system with the commissions I was being charged, so I concentrated more Jacob's macro views.

While my admiration of Jacob grew, my trust of Bill dwindled. For a time, I'd play it cool with Bill until I could move my business away from him.

My last morning in Florida, Jacob revealed it was his idea for me to remain in a holding pattern until into the third week of the sideways market. He believed over the next few days, the market was primed for a big rally. I liked that. I'd steadily increased position size up to this point, remembering some of the first words Bill ever said to me back in April: "Another consideration is to add positions on to make up the losses quicker." Riding out the storm a little longer seemed more appealing now.

I trusted Jacob's advice and thought about what it could mean if the market rallied with just the contracts I had open. I was in a long position and large position. If the market rallied like Jacob believed, the profit still wouldn't bring me out of the hole with my current contracts.

When I returned home, it was time for one of those load-the-wagon trades Jacob had advised. Full of confidence, I told Bill I wanted 200 contracts. His eyes twinkled behind his magnified glasses. I could tell the thought of $60 commissions on two hundred contracts made his heart flutter.

"If Jacob's right, this could be what you've been waiting for," he said.

I detected a bit of feigned concern but he wasn't about to hold me back. I was not only a player, but a huge player now. I loved the rush of running with the big boys.

Within a few days, Jacob proved his acumen. The market took off in the last week of August. Prior to the market surge, we sat in a holding pattern, up one day and down the next, a frustrating experience for a newbie. I struggled with how to handle something out my control. Insecurity set in about my decisions. I second guessed those decisions more times than I care to remember. Then the market started to move in my direction. By the end of the month, I was galloping out of the hole. With all the boneheaded moves of the prior four months and the number of long contracts I had, the market jumped and took my debt down to

$65,000. That's still a lot of money, but certainly a relief from July's low point of almost $300,000.

I closed 272 contracts and kept 220 open. Again insanely leveraged. Among those contracts were 114 hog contracts and fifty cattle options. There was a realized loss of $6,845 but the amount of open profits I had on the books was simply huge. It looked like this thing might finally turn around.

Professionally things were looking up. Personally, that was another story. Despite the stress of dealing with an up-and-down market, one area of my life remained constant—my tumultuous relationship with Tammy. I endured her manipulation and accusations of cheating for much longer than I should. When I broke it off, she bolted to Mexico with friends. While Tammy was away, I met and dated another girl for a while. After she returned, Tammy wormed her way back into my life. I ended the other relationship because I didn't, and still don't, believe in dating two women at once.

The morning I left for Florida, Tammy thought she caught me cheating when she answered the phone when the other girl called. Tammy didn't say a word until I called her the night before I was to return home.

She answered with, "You sure you didn't mean to call Tina?"

We argued and I ended the fight by hanging up. And prayed she wouldn't call back.

But just as soon as things looked up professionally, the market took another nose dive. I didn't know how much longer I could take it. I wanted my life back. The stability of attending classes, hanging out with friends, and having a steady non-volcanic relationship.

August rolled into September, and after loading up with contracts at the end of August, per Jacob's advice, I watched—excitedly—my gargantuan position move in the right direction. Finally. At the close of business, Wednesday, September 3, the debt was almost gone. I don't recall ever feeling the euphoria I felt that night. We were almost out of hole.

The next day I walked into Bill's office and looked at the board. Then at Bill and Fred.

"It's back," I whispered. "The account is all back."

Fred grinned and fiddled with his tie. "And then some I think."

He knew my positions as well I did. I went to the books and checked the math I had just done in my head. I was several thousand dollars in the green, after even my dad's losses.

In all the years since, I have tried to come up with the words I felt at that moment. To me, it's one of those moments you have to experience to understand. A moment in a person's life in which something monstrously good overcomes months of setback after setback.

I grabbed my jacket and headed out the door. The day had become too beautiful to sit in the office. Too overcome to even celebrate, I simply stared at the road on the drive to my apartment. I got home and called my dad.

"We're clear, Dad," I said.

"What?"

I spoke the next words just above a whisper. "The account's positive. All our losses have been made up. Plus a few grand." After Dad screamed a word of jubilation, I added. "We did it. It's finally over."

Months of nail biting, finger crossing, toe crossing even, now done. Over with.

"*You* did it, Tiger!"

The emphasis on the first word overwhelmed me. I don't recall ever hearing that tone of excitement from my dad.

"Well, it was really luck more than anything, dad," I said. "That guy in Florida really gave me some good advice."

"You're the one who made the trades. I knew you wouldn't let me down."

"First thing in the morning I'm going to sell the entire position."

"Whoa there, Buddy. Why do that now?"

"I'm exhausted. I need a *long* vacation. I can't tell you how stressful this has been."

"Have you thought this through? Taken some time—"

"I've done nothing but think about this. Trust me."

"Before you say another word I want you to hang up," he said, getting serious. "Then go down to the nearest Corvette dealer. Pick yourself out the prettiest car you've ever laid eyes on. That will be my gift to you for all of your amazing efforts."

A Corvette sounded like a wonderful idea. Dad knew I had always wanted one and a new car would be a bright, silver lining to the hellish, dark cloud. "You're serious?" I asked.

He was and told me to call him from the dealership. I was drained, but the thought of looking at Corvettes infused some energy into my weary body. I sat on my bed for a minute staring at the wall, then jumped up, grabbed my keys, and drove to the dealership.

I narrowed my choices to a loaded, cherry red '83 model and a yellow '84 with a Doug Nash "4+3" transmission. That gave me another shot of energy. Man, all that horsepower underneath me. Much better than my 1982 Toyota Supra.

I couldn't get my dad's words out of my mind: "*You* did it, Tiger!" The more I thought, the more I realized, I had done nothing. I had blundered my way into a positive position eventually. Dad had no idea how the account had become positive, nor did he care. He had given me responsibility and trusted that I could handle anything.

After putting my family through all I had, getting a new car suddenly didn't feel right. I knew it had been blind luck. I left the dealership feeling tired, worn out, and like a fake. I called my dad and told him I didn't buy the car and "first thing in the morning, I am selling everything."

"Listen to me," he said. "It's not just about the car. I've been thinking...." he paused, and I waited. "Maybe this is something you want to do."

"What do you mean?"

"Trading, boy," he said. "Seems like you know how to make some real money doing this stuff. And Steve, you know there are some people who think this market's going higher, right?" He planted a seed in my mind.

"What about the cattle trading?"

"Oh heck, don't you worry about that. You'll be doing just fine, and so will I." If he was serious, this was a game changer. I was not in love with trading by any stretch of the imagination, but Dad had just offered me what sounded like a golden ticket. The chance to not be stuck in Ponderosa was a carrot I couldn't resist. I did not cherish the idea of driving 80,000 miles a year like he did. I wanted to be with my future wife and kids, sleeping soundly in the wee hours of the morning, and not closing deals in a dirty, dusty corral.

"Dad," I said. "That's not a bad idea."

Funny how a person's emotions can flip in a heartbeat. I imagined myself driving a Corvette I'd purchased on my own, with trophy girlfriends hanging onto my every word as I got better and better at trading. And richer and richer. I could get my license, even talk to Jacob and see if I could emulate his strategy. I could be a high roller. In a bigger city than Ponderosa. I talked more with my dad and said numerous times how proud he was. I felt great again.

"What about the account?" I asked.

"Well, take tomorrow and the weekend, and see what you want to do. Like I said, many of these cattlemen are talking about it going really high. It's up to you though. You're the pro." He laughed, and I got that uneasy feeling again.

I took Friday off and spent the day relaxing, and thinking about the mayhem of the previous few months. Dad wanted me to keep trading but he just didn't understand how fortunate we were to be positive, and he certainly didn't understand how the trades had worked. Given my lack of experience, it really was nothing short of a miracle. But then again, I couldn't really blame him because he believed in something that was a facade.

Several times throughout that day I thought it best to sell. To get out while things were good. I could've used a few days, even weeks, of recovery from the emotional hell of trading full-time. On the plus side, I could leave Ponderosa, make hundreds of thousands of dollars, and buy my 'Vette. All that sounded nice.

I woke up on Saturday feeling restless. That feeling continued for the weekend. With the exception of the words with my dad about Emily, I never stood up to him. I needed to again. I really needed a break. Cash out with the money good, and come back later when I felt fresh. I called dad and told him my plan. I'd close out positions and wire the money into his account. After that call, I was able to relax the rest of the weekend.

On Monday morning I strode into Bill's office ready to sell. Everyone seemed subdued.

"They're calling cattle to open down seventy-five cents to a buck," Fred said, without expression. After four months of learning to calculate instantly how much I'd lose, I knew for every buck, it would cost me $400 per contract. I multiplied that by my open contracts and I was looking at being down over $100,000 right off the bat. I nearly threw up.

I sat and buried my face in my hands. My world closed in on me. How could this be? Was this the life of a trader? If so, I definitely wanted out. I was being dragged back down, into that deep, dark tunnel of relentless stress and dread. I clawed at the sides of the tunnel, and tried to protest, but almost threw up again. After a second try I managed a hoarse, "What do you think, Bill?"

He suggested we put my orders just under Friday's close and see if they'd come back and fill us up. I knew what he was aiming for. Many times a market will open lower and rally back near the prior day's close. If we placed our sell orders just below Friday's close then maybe the market might go up enough to execute our orders. As much as I hated to at this point, I took Bill's advice and we waited for the market to open.

It did open sharply lower. I was more scared this time than any other. I think, after my week with Jacob Sarno, the leverage I was dealing with had finally sunken in. I kept doing the same, maddening calculation over and over again. Three hundred contracts down only $1, equals $120,000.

While I silently pleaded with God, I sat behind Fred and stared at that big mechanical quote board. Every time the cattle made a new low, the sound grew louder as the last price, and the new low rolled over together. The flips of the mechanical numbers crashed down like the sound of an imploding skyscraper. Time and time again, the new low smashed into the old, thundering through the room. Eventually, to keep my sanity I got up and staggered out to the bathroom. I knew it was pointless, but I had to try to escape somehow, even for a minute.

I walked back into the office and the market was down another twenty-five cents. I almost laughed at the horrible joke being played on me. I computed how costly that bathroom break was. One hundred dollars per contract, times three hundred. Only $30,000 lost in five minutes.

The rest of day I fought an internal battle between fighting off panic and staving off throwing up. I detached myself from the situation. Finally, I pleaded with God to save me again. Lord, this time I really mean it, I will change.

As if time stopped, everything crystallized into the most profoundly lucid realization. I recalled my prayer several weeks earlier. It was the same prayer. Save me Lord and I will turn my life around. I didn't. I went back to my favorite God—hedonism. I saw I was entirely consumed by lust, and I lived to party with whichever friends I pleased.

I gave zero time to God, except in these moments when fear and panic were about to suffocate me. The trading stress felt like a feather compared to how my guilt crushed down upon me. I had broken my promise to God. He kept His end of the deal I offered, He did the impossible and made a way for my contracts to get into the black. But I got greedy, and now found myself in a deeper hole.

I looked over at the clock. Thirty minutes to go. The market had stopped moving. It was down a full $1.00, but at least it wasn't getting worse. Could God be showing me mercy yet again? Even now. After all this? The market just needs to hold in here, I thought. Then I'll have time to figure out what to do tomorrow. I barely blinked as my eyes bored into the quotes. I had never experienced an eternity until then. Every minute was a thousand years. The market continued to drop a few cents, every few minutes, taking my peace with it. It dropped all the way to $1.20. In the last minute the market rallied fifteen cents. My loss for the day came to $127,000.

Chapter 9

WHEN YOU HIT
ROCK BOTTOM ...

A fter that first week of September, the market went down. And down again. And down just a little bit more. Watching my account lose tens of thousands of dollars a day drove my spirits into the abyss. Why didn't I sell when we were in the green? Greed, I guess. Then the market avalanched. Every slight rise gave me a flutter of false hope that made the subsequent drop twice as bitter. I felt trapped. And paralyzed. I just couldn't bring myself to pull the trigger and eat the losses.

After Dad bailed me out earlier, I didn't know how I could explain that we took more losses. I begged God to turn around the market. I didn't care how. I just wanted things, even a four-cent boost, to turn in our favor. I promised God that I'd change my life and be obedient to Him. I vowed to stop drinking and partying. No matter how much I pleaded, the market slide continued.

I also had begun to have doubts about Bill. In July, based on his advice, I loaded up on huge positions and leverage our account to the max with more than 200 contracts. Years later, I realized he was worried about his liability, probably more so than my account.

By comparison, my dad's first trade was a five-contract lot, very small and conservative. When he got caught in the dairy buyout program, he averaged in a few times, a strategy to make up a loss by buying twice as many contracts to make the difference back. He never let his lots get out of hand, something I wished I'd done too.

When I took over, we'd do fifty lots on a regular basis. That grew to 100 and eventually to the 200. Not a wise move, for sure. And, which there shouldn't have been an 'and,' I also had options and a few hogs. This brought my total to nearly three-hundred contracts, which meant a small one dollar move was equal to $120,000, plus or minus. My dad's trading account was down less than $100,000 when I took over and at the end of July, it was approaching $250,000 in the red.

Looking back, I should not have been that active, or even in the market. I received ridiculous advice over and over and over. Get in. Get out. Buy options. Sell options. Reverse positions. Reverse again. My head felt like that one of those little spinning toys we played with as a child. Bill encouraged me to go with size (large lots) to make up for losses in a hurry. I didn't realize, or maybe I didn't know, that he received $60 per trade, per contract.

One night Bill and his wife Sally took me out to dinner. His wife, Sally, a short, somewhat rotund, upbeat and jovial lady with snow white hair, was always neatly dressed, in contrast to Bill, who generally seemed sad. Bill and Sally preferred to dine out to eating a home. At the restaurant I discovered why. Bill, ever the salesman, was a master of the time-tested client retention drill: dine at a fancy restaurant, get the client liquored up on the most expensive poisons, and show the client that a partnership will be successful, luxurious and decadent. Bill gave me a heavy pitch that night. Sally chimed in with encouragement to trust her husband.

A heavy drinker, Sally increased her intake that night. After dinner she threw up in her hand, tossed it on the floor, and wiped her hand on her napkin. I wanted to throw up myself. How could someone do something so repulsive? I think my disgust showed. Bill ripped into Sally, which led to a huge fight. While they argued, I learned their empire might be on the verge of crumbling.

About a month later, Fred Willoughby took me out, and in no uncertain terms, told me that I might want to consider getting out sooner rather than later. That's all he could say without breaching legal restraints. Fred also confirmed that things weren't good at Bill Black Commodities.

I wanted to get out. I had for a while, but feared my dad's reaction to the massive loss. If I cut my losses with Bill, I'd have to absorb huge losses... and have to explain that to my dad. Thank goodness I had Fred to lean on. I no longer trusted Bill. Studying how to trade helped, but I still had much to learn, like learning to use common sense and trust my instincts.

This kind of stress cripples a person into uncertainty. You second guess, triple guess, quadruple guess every thought, every decision. Sleep becomes evasive. Food really does lose its taste.

The next week, the market dropped again. With it went my hopes of ever getting back to even. I drank more. Every day those numbers on the board crashed down into new, more abysmal lows. I could barely keep calculating my losses. Some days I didn't want to. I stuck with my huge, long-shot positions. My only chance was to wait for the next wave, which never came.

Bill delivered the bad news in his office early one morning. "You're on a margin call of $150,000." He couldn't look me in the eye. "We are going to need a wire today."

I still had my positions open, and spread out like this was the proverbial death from a thousand cuts. The account had gone from green to more than $400,000 down. The margin money was wiped out with nothing left to carry the positions. There wasn't even any liquidity left in the business to margin up. I was sunk.

"I know," I said. I flashed back to July when I had convinced my dad to wire more than $200,000 and promised him it would work out. "Trust me Dad." The words echoed hauntingly in my mind. I told my dad I wanted out. I told him I wanted to sell. Why had he placed doubt in my mind?

"Steve?" Bill snapped me back to the present.

I could barely swallow. "Sell everything." Before Bill could respond, I turned and left.

I had to tell my dad. I probably should have driven home. But with tears pouring down my face, I wouldn't have made the two-hour drive. Instead, I drove to my apartment to make the worst call in my life.

I let my dad down, probably in the worst way possible. I told him that I'd fix this. And I failed. It didn't matter that I was just twenty-two years old and with little experience in this arena. I told him I'd save the day. Boy was I fool.

I tried rehearsing the conversation. No words seem the right words, or the right order. I gave up on putting together the perfect "I screwed up, Dad" speech. I arrived home and went to straight to the phone. I wiped my eyes, took a deep breath, and dialed my dad's number at work.

"Sterling Livestock," the receptionist said.

My heartbeat doubled, maybe tripled. Forget breathing at this point. Just wasn't happening.

"Jack Meyers, please."

"Just a moment."

I prayed, "Please God, get me through this." And I reminded myself that I could get through this. Be strong. Be a man.

My father's voice boomed a greeting.

Instantly, I drained my well of emotion. The fear. The stress. The anguish. Everything that I had held back for the past four months gushed out in huge sobs.

Dad's voice boomed again. "Hello?"

Just make a noise I thought to myself. "Dad...."

"Tiger, is that you?"

"Yes," I croaked.

"Are you okay?"

"It's gone, dad, it's all gone." There. I made progress. I can do this. "I had to sell out."

The silence crushed me. "Dad?"

"I don't know," he finally screamed, "what the hell to tell you."

The floor under me drifted away. I grasped for something—anything—to grasp. His reaction was worse than I thought.

Far worse.

Chapter 10

THE SLIDE CONTINUES

I gotta go," my dad said.

And just like that, my career as a trader, thankfully, was over.

We closed 593 contracts in September. All remaining positions were liquidated because we couldn't come up with a cash infusion. Our losses totaled more than $400,000. The uncertainty of what might happen next kept me up for four hours staring at the wall until I nodded off from exhaustion.

A few days later I ventured out to a sports bar. There, I ran into another Bill Black client, Nathan Hickerson. A tall, distinguished gentleman when I met him at Black's office, he looked the same on the outside—wearing a smoker's jacket and bolo tie. But now, he looked tired and old. I soon found out why. He'd lost everything. "Well, I never want to speak badly of anyone," Nathan said, "but you know old Bill Black, he wasn't the best guy to do business with."

I couldn't argue with that. I liked Nathan, and my heart broke for him. Worse, I was terrified at ending up on a bar stool at his age with no money to my name.

Of course, with the positions liquidated, we closed the account at Bill Black Commodities. I felt very angry at myself and Bill Black. I was in way over my head. I took Bill's advice over and over again. Ultimately, I was responsible as I signed off on the trades but I felt Bill should never have let the position size get so out of hand. There was no room for error. Excessive commissions also drained the account.

I ping ponged between being relieved the account was wiped out and depressed knowing I'd lost my parents' life work. My dad and I never talked about the loss, but we did talk more. Before the crash, we'd talk maybe two or three times a week. After, we talked every day, it seemed. Still usually about work. During one of those conversations, I realized from his tone—one that I hated as a child—he was "pushing me" again. He still believed I could be a success. I needed that from him.

During another talk, I gathered the courage to ask him how they were getting by. Dad explained that because of his outstanding banking record, reputation and character, he was able to secure a loan that enabled him to stay afloat. The loan wasn't the half-a-million dollar cash net worth he'd accumulated—and I'd lost.

At least he could survive. That wasn't good enough, though. My parents deserved more than just to survive. Dad didn't deserve to drink a lesser known brand of beer. Mom didn't deserve to sparsely fill the fridge. I made a promise to myself to make this right.

We decided to try our luck with another brokerage firm and scraped together what money we could to install a quote system in my apartment in Glacier. After the devastating loss, I didn't want to be seen by anybody. Staying in every day would be a huge relief while I put my life back together. Deep down, I doubted I could pull it off. In my moments of despair, knowing we'd bounced back from $300,000 kept me going.

At the recommendation of a friend, we went with a brokerage owned by Rachel Owens. Her approach to the markets with an educated and technical analysis contrasted Black's way of relying on fundamental news. Her way better suited our goals. Still sick from losing my parents' money, she and I agreed that she'd call me if she got a signal from her indicators, or I'd call her if I thought I saw an opportunity. We began buying twenty-five or fifty contracts of live cattle or hogs.

Through November we won some and lost some, pretty typical for trading. Young and anxious, I wanted a quicker return and decided to step up my game in December. This turned out to be a huge mistake, another in a series that nearly wiped out my sanity in the coming months.

By now, the markets had absorbed the news of the dairy buyout, as well as Chernobyl. This meant no more huge moves up or down, but rather that sideways, choppy action. I got somewhat out of sync with the markets and, going it alone without advice from Bill or Jacob, I made some bad decisions. Heavy losses piled up and I lost most of my working capital.

The weight on my shoulders grew heavier by the day. Christmas was around the corner. I didn't look forward to sharing more bad news with my parents over the holidays. Some nights I'd bolt upright in a cold sweat, begging for it all to be a horrible nightmare. It never was.

The markets were my companion by day with the quote machine my warden. That wretched quote machine. Seeing it when I woke up—and when I went to bed—reminded me over and over and over of all my mistakes.

The numbers showed each day that I could not recoup the money I'd lost. I tried so hard to do something I simply was not qualified, nor experienced enough, to do. This quest ended months ago. I knew it. I just didn't have the guts to admit it to anyone else. I hated myself and I hated every new day. Each day I awoke to a fresh sense of dread.

What a life. Over at age twenty-two. Destined to chase a dream I could never catch. And probably live in squalor until death claimed me.

For Christmas break, I packed Tammy and Tabitha up for the trip home to fake my happiness in front of Mom and Dad for a week before I dropped another bomb on their life. We arrived in Ponderosa, and my parents were thrilled to see us. We hugged, reminisced, wrapped presents, and drank cocoa, trying to make it all special for Tabitha. For a day or so I lived the perfect illusion of a picturesque, extended family, celebrating the holidays.

A few nights into the trip, Tammy and I met friends at a bar across the railroad tracks, about a city block from my parents' home. About 1:00 a.m., after more drinks than I can remember, Tammy, a surprising comfort in my darkest hour despite the drinking and fighting, overheard a woman tell Shawn and I that she wanted to take us back to her place. Tammy stormed into the cold winter night, furious.

By the time I got across the tracks Tammy, barely able to stand, was fumbling with Tabitha's car seat.

"What the heck are you doing?" I asked.

"Driving back to Glacier you pig."

"You are not driving over two hundred miles, in your condition, with your child in the car."

Tammy started yelling, using a lot of unprintable words, and I feared she might wake my parents. She got her daughter buckled up and plopped into the driver's seat.

"Don't be ridiculous," I said. "Let's just go back in to the house and sleep it off. We can talk about it in the morning."

This pushed her over the edge. The intensity and volume of her outburst rose a few notches. She accused me of sleeping with the woman at the bar. That accusation flew often when she drank too much, although I never cheated on her.

During her rant, she closed the driver's door. I leaned through the window and tried to grab the keys. I couldn't let her drive home. Not with Tabitha in the car. I'm pretty sure they wouldn't have made it back to Glacier. Tammy beat on my arm with more strength than I realized she had. I kept trying for the keys and she kept beating back my attempt.

Lights flashing, a police car pulled into the driveway. Good. Maybe the cop could convince Tammy to stay. I stood up. The officer threw open his door and walked straight for me. I knew this guy, Alex Harris. I'd been good friends with his brother throughout high school.

I greeted him, but he bristled and barked, "Exactly what are you doing?"

"What do you mean?"

"Punching her in the face."

His tone concerned me, as did he glare. "I wasn't punching her."

Harris kept his eyes trained on me while sliding his hand to his holster. He stepped over to the window and glanced inside at Tammy. His suspicious look told me this wasn't going the way I hoped.

"Listen," I said, respectfully. "All my girlfriend and I want to do is go in the house and talk this out. There is no problem here." I didn't want to get Tammy arrested if I could help it. Sitting in her car was enough to get a DUI.

"I can tell you hit her in the nose. Stay back." He narrowed his eyes. "Do you understand me?"

I did not hit Tammy. If I had, blood would've covered her face. He didn't see that, only what he wanted. A girl he could rescue, for whatever reason. Harris ordered Tammy out of her car and into his cruiser. She gave me a death stare before following him. While he interviewed Tammy, I checked on Tabitha. She seemed scared. I couldn't blame her. First seeing her mother and boyfriend fighting and then seeing a pushy cop. Frankly, I was scared too. I sat in the car with Tabitha and turned on the heater for her.

While waiting for Harris to return with Tammy and tell me everything was okay, I remembered his questionable reputation. I was the one in trouble, not Tammy. Rumors persisted about an alliance between Harris and the county attorney. In a little place like Ponderosa, that quickly turned into small-town law.

After about twenty minutes, I left Tammy's car, walked over to his, opened the door, said, "What in the hell is going on man?"

Not the right thing to say. Harris exploded out of the vehicle and hit me in the sternum with his shoulder. I landed on the ground, face first. He leaped on me, grabbed my wrist, and wrenched my arm up so high behind my back it made my eyes water.

He arrested me and took me to the jail. I'd never been jailed before. I think we all have certain expectations based on what we've seen on television and in the movies. But sitting on a bench with those bars separating you from the outside world gives a person a different perspective. I experienced a moment of "is this really happening?" Coupled with the rumors about the arresting officer, I wasn't sure what to expect next. Different scenarios flitted through my mind and I feared the worst.

Fifteen minutes later, I heard a commotion at the door of the cell. I looked up. My dad. Not the person I wanted to see at this moment.

"What's going on?" he asked, sleep and concern heavy in his eyes.

I felt terrible. I couldn't imagine the thoughts running through his mind. Or worse, what Tammy had told him. I recounted my version of the story. Then I cried for the first I could remember in front of my dad, a man's man. Crying was the sign of weakness to him. And here I was, crying and blubbering like a little boy.

"Is this about the commodities?"

Yes, but I didn't want to ruin Christmas by telling him the money was gone forever with no chance of recovering it.

"Don't lie to me. Is all this about the commodities?"

"You know, I really don't think I want to trade anymore." There. I said it. After just five months in a job that usually takes a person five years to master, I wanted out. And now he knew it too.

"You can't give up on me now buddy. Can you?"

I'm sure he didn't know, but those words were the most crushing thing I'd heard in my life. I sat there stunned. I didn't know what to say. I had gone from a being somewhat relieved to having more pressure heaped on me. Again.

"Steve?" My name pulled me from staring into space. I thought he wanted a response. Instead he continued, "They're not going to let you out on bail."

They didn't because charges weren't filed yet. Dad confronted Harris about this. A loud argument ensued in which my dad was slapped with a disorderly charge. I wanted to laugh, to bring relief to the situation, but I worried about what might happen next. I heard the station door slam. Dad must have left.

How could have things spiraled so out of control that I now sat on a crappy bed in a jail cell in my hometown? I dropped my head into my hands. Why were these things happening to me? I had done nothing wrong. I know, just about every person in jail says something similar. All I wanted was to keep Tammy from driving away with Tabitha. Yet, I felt like the lowlife.

Now, Dad was in trouble. I wouldn't allow myself to think about my mother's reaction. I couldn't. I'd start crying again. Instead I focused on what my dad said. Big mistake. His words, "You can't give up on me now ... You can't give up on me now..." ricocheted around the caverns of my mind.

I shut my eyes. Thankfully, the room spun only at half speed.

Chapter 11

A SHIVER
DOWN MY SPINE

My dad drove home, called Judge Hollis, a friend, at 3:00 a.m., and explained the ordeal with Officer Harris in the driveway.

"Bail him out and we'll take a look tomorrow," the judge said.

"They won't charge him," Dad said, "or haven't charged him yet, so no bail. I protested and the cop charged me with disorderly conduct."

After a few seconds, Hollis sighed. "If it's Steve it can't be that bad."

"What can we do? If I go down there again, I'll kick someone's butt up between their ears."

Dad said Hollis waited a moment before he said, "I'll call them and instruct they release him on $500 bond. But Jack, I want Steve before me at 9:00 a.m. sharp."

The next morning, Dad and I arrived early. We strode through doors of the two-story brick building, around the open area in the center of the first floor where a few desks sat, past the office for the county attorney, past one of the sheriffs, and into Judge Hollis's office. He beat us there. Before we sat and he handed me the police report with raised eyebrows.

I eased into a chair across the desk from him and read through the charges. I laughed out loud at the some of the comments in the report: "Officer observed victim's nose broken. Victim bleeding and scratched. Smashed holding cell observation camera?"

None of this was true. Not a single word. I wanted to find Harris and punch out his lights, as well as some of the other cops who must have been in on it for Harris to claim I smashed the camera.

"Judge, this is unbelievable." I slammed the report onto the desk. "None of this is true."

"Those are some serious charges," he said in a voice I'm sure he had used numerous times to defuse a victim's anger. "How do you explain them?"

I could tell he wanted to believe me, but the black and white ink on the page shouted some frightening allegations. "Judge, they're simply not true. There isn't a scratch on my girlfriend. I was trying to prevent her from breaking the law. Not trying to break it myself."

The judge looked over at my dad and clenched his jaw. "Domestic abuse, resisting arrest, criminal mischief. This is no joke."

"Judge," my dad said, "with all due respect, I sure as hell am not laughing. I believe Steve. He may have protested when he was arrested, but I know he isn't stupid enough to have fought back." My dad turned to me. "Right?"

"Is the girl still in town?" the judge said.

"She's at our house right now," Dad said.

"Bring her down here. And tell her not to wear makeup."

I waited in the judge's chambers and we passed the time with small talk. Dad returned a little while later with Tammy, who showed up sans makeup as instructed. Tammy took a seat across the desk from Hollis. I sat in the chair next to her. Dad stood in the background while the judge asked questions and looked Tammy over.

"Were you fighting?" he asked.

"Yeah... I guess." Tammy shifted in her seat. "Nothing to warrant all this though."

I realized I had been holding my breath, and exhaled. This was her chance to bury me, and she didn't take it. For the first time since the fight started at the bar, I felt Tammy might actually be on my side.

"Can you show me your arms please?"

Tammy held her arms out.

"Tell me honestly... did Mr. Meyers Junior lay hands on you in an abusive manner in any way?"

"No, sir. He did not."

I could have kissed her right there. It was evident she didn't have a mark on her, but she could have still tried to burn me. I had a hunch she wouldn't though, once she was sober. That was usually the sequence of events.

The judge rubbed his face. "Steve, I'm really sorry you had to go through all of this. Quite frankly, I'm furious."

"Thank you so much, sir." An invisible weight suffocating me evaporated.

"This is absolutely ridiculous." The look in his eyes revealed his anger toward the situation. "I will get this case dismissed and try to get Harris dismissed too." He glanced over at Tammy again, eyeing her arms and face, and shook his head.

After my dad voiced his thankfulness, the judge said, "It will take a little red tape, but I will get this case dismissed. You'll have to give a sworn statement before you leave though." He nodded toward Tammy. "I recommend taking some pictures of Tammy too."

"Thank you again, your honor." I said, and Tammy did the same.

That night, Tammy and I went to the sheriff's office to give our sworn statements. We felt pretty good about our meeting earlier with Judge Hollis. I didn't see any way Harris could press charges at this point.

When we walked in, Harris sat at the table, across from the woman who'd take our statements. I sat next to him and Tammy next to me. The way Harris looked at Tammy annoyed me, as if they had some history together due to his interrogation. He didn't seem fazed we were about to give sworn statements that would contradict his report.

While we gave our statements, we struck up a conversation with the dispatcher and discovered that she, like Tammy, lived in Glacier. At one point,

Harris interrupted and before he said much, I cut him off. "Let me tell you one thing, you have messed with the wrong person." The never-back-down attitude my dad instilled kept me strong in the face of this atrocious person. "I swear on everything dear to me, I will not let this go."

I wanted to hit him. Instead, I started a stare down the dispatcher interrupted. "Harris, go wait outside, okay?"

The holidays were a little subdued after that, but we tried to keep our spirits up for Tabitha's sake. Judge Hollis moved to dismiss, but while paperwork moved through the system, the hearing was set for March.

After Christmas, I bid my parents, particularly my dad, an emotional farewell. We drove home to Glacier. Tammy and I didn't talk much. Tabitha slept most of the way. The closer we got, the more stress I felt about my recent failings in the market. The quote machine in my apartment greeted me with a deathly, hollow stare. Good to be home. I guess.

Chapter 12
THE BOTTOM, FOR REAL

S oon after we returned home, I learned the case had not been dropped. I guess Officer Harris didn't know when to back down. Along with giving a sworn statement that I did hit Tammy, he and the country attorney would not drop chargers against my dad.

With this hanging over my head, I couldn't concentrate on the markets. I fought so many mental battles that I physically wore myself out. A week later, I realized I couldn't get the money back. I'd dug too big a hole. Mentally, I sunk even further into a corner of my mind where I hoped to feel safe.

My dad had made it clear he wanted me to keep trading. I felt I could. He didn't raise a quitter, and I wasn't about to cash in, or rather cash out. I knew I'd made a lot of mistakes. We all do. In some jobs, a mistake might go unnoticed or have little effect on a project. In trading, a mistake can cost a person hundreds of thousands of dollars. And I had done that. Twice now.

To help deal with my losses, I often laid awake for endless hours, my mind my worst enemy. After nights of this stretched into weeks, I made a habit of walking through the neighborhoods of Glacier. With the average February low in the teens, wandering seemed the best way to clear my head.

At first I stayed on my street, an older established neighborhood, for a few trips back and forth. Even with a parka, I could feel the biting cold. If I woke up in a panic, like this night, and had to get out and walk, sometimes I wouldn't be dressed properly with the right shoes and gloves.

When it seemed no one was awake to see me trudging, head down, through the neighborhood, I expanded my wayward excursion into nearby developments. I walked for hours, usually right in the middle of the road. Light from the street lamps reflected off the snow-packed roads while I kept my head down against the cold and wind. I asked God to rescue me from this emotional hell.

I replayed what had transpired the last couple of months and asked over and over, how did I get here? This wasn't me? How could I let this happen? The proverbial punch in the gut came with each question until I couldn't ask any longer. I switched to "Oh my God, oh my God," Despite the frigid weather, I felt as if I was in hell.

A few days later, I anticipated a down turn in the market. This gave me a glimmer of hope. I ignored my insanely over-leveraged positions and loaded up one more time, hopefully the last. It may seem strange to think I could do anything so risky again. At this point, it was all just paper money. $10,000 made here, $20,000 lost there. The equivalent of a used Corvette one week, then made up the next.

Rachel, my new broker called. I grabbed the phone while lying in bed. She didn't sound happy. "Are you aware your account is deeply in the red?"

Her panic annoyed and scared me at the same time.

"Uhh... yeah, I'm pretty aware of that."

"You have a negative balance of $70,000 in your account." I'm going to need the money right away."

"Hold on a second." I didn't like her antsy tone. "This just happened okay. You know that. I don't have the money right at this moment." My tone changed to placate her instead of pissing her off. "I'm going to need a little time, but I will get it to you soon. I promise."

"Soon won't do. I cannot carry that amount of cash as a favor. I need it today. Your positions are going to be liquidated anyway."

I told her I couldn't pay her today, and despite her saying I was a good kid and she liked me, we had a little tiff about when I could get her the money. Nothing like being strong-armed while hung over.

"If I don't have a check on this desk tomorrow, I'll be forced to begin a legal process against you."

I was offended, but beginning to freak out. This was new territory. For more times than I can remember, when I thought it couldn't get any worse, it did.

The phone rang again. Rachel Owens's legal representation, Debbie White, this time. "Rachel tells me you are refusing to pay a large sum of money you owe?"

"That's not true." I realized too late I'd been baited into talking.

"It's not important how you get the money. You made the trades. Rachel took your account on good faith, and you are responsible for your trades." Her voice was thin and mean. "It is imperative you get a check to Rachel by tomorrow, for the full amount, or we will have to take severe action."

"I. Do. Not. Have. It. What more can I tell you?"

The phone was silent for a few seconds, adding to my anxiety. "As I said, it is your responsibility to maintain the cash in reserves for every trade you make. It is highly unfortunate you haven't followed trading protocol. I will have no choice but to file for a warrant to arrest and hold you until you can make the payment."

"What?" I blurted. "Are you crazy?"

"I assure you I am not, sir."

"Ah, c'mon. There is no way you can have me arrested for not having the money right away."

"Try me."

I could tell she'd be up for the challenge, might even enjoy it.

"I'm hanging up now. If Ms. Hall doesn't have the money tomorrow, do not leave the city or state. Do you understand?"

"Whatever." I bluffed and hung up on her.

I shook. I didn't want to go to jail. I couldn't go to jail, not after what I experienced at Christmas. I didn't think I could have sunk any lower, but the abyss just got a little deeper, the hole a little bigger.

I knew Dad kept about $100,000 in the corporate account for his cattle trading cash flow. I still had a checkbook and wrote a check to cover my losses. I drove to Rachel's office, threw the check on the table, and asked her if she could wait a day to deposit. I wanted to figure out a way to tell my dad. She said no. I nearly flipped her off.

I went straight home. I think I sat in a catatonic state on my couch for about twelve hours. Only God knows what ran through my mind during the time. I don't think it mattered because only one thing did: I must make another devastating call to my dad.

The next day he answered with a warm "Yello?"

My greeting carried the nervousness of a ten-year-old in trouble, and he picked up on it.

"What's up buddy?"

I got right to the point. "I made some long trades, and the market went exactly opposite. I lost it all."

"Are you kidding me, son?" He was clearly getting tired of hearing this. I sat waiting for him to say something because I didn't have anything else to share. "Not again." This was bad, his tone not like him. Then something must have clicked. "Was it just the working capital?"

"No, dad. It's a lot worse."

The silence terrified me. "How much worse?"

"I wrote a check for $70,000 from the corporate account to cover the margin call."

"You did *what?*" I was too scared to say another word. "Why in the hell would you do such a thing? Are you kidding me right now, boy?"

"I had to." I tried to defend my actions, but the words sounded silly when they came out of my mouth. "They were about to have me arrested."

"Arrested? What else is there to the story?"

"Nothing, I swear," I could feel myself backpedaling now. "Rachel's lawyer called me and said by not having the funds, I was breaking trading protocol, and she was going to have me arrested and hold me until I could pay."

"Aw shoot, that's a load of hogcrap. You believed her? That's just strong-arming tactics"

"I panicked. I'm sorry, Dad. I didn't know what to do."

"Why didn't you just come talk to me son?" I hadn't heard my dad this upset in a long time. "Where the hell am I going to get the money from now? Those funds have been pledged to the bank for a cattle loan. Do you know what you've done?"

Crap. I spent money my dad promised to someone else. I had become accustomed to doing things on my own, like most guys my age, and didn't think to talk first with my dad. His panic devastated me. I wanted to cry, but didn't want to shame him with my tears.

"It's over," he said, barely above a whisper, "it's all done."

I understood the finality, but couldn't go down without a fight. But I didn't have the words.

He repeated his last statement and hung up.

"Steve, this is over." He hung up.

Dad got it. Sooner than me. He trusted a twenty-two-year-old rookie, and lost. Nothing remained. And if he had nothing left, I had less than nothing.

Everything pent up from the past year erupted in a long wail. I feel to my knees and sobbed harder than a grown man should. Hot tears flooded my cheeks. Shame and guilt and despair crept over me like a shadowy fog. I groaned and tore at my hair.

My emotions seesawed between anger at myself and despair for my family's future. I fell into the fetal position. The disappointment in my dad's voice rang in my ears. It's over. It was true. For me, the world was over. Everything my family had, our entire way of life, our family, would never be the same again.

I couldn't handle letting down my dad. I needed to explain how we got into this position, how crazy trading was, how unequipped I was. I knew he'd understand. But more than that, I needed him to forgive me.

I sat up, wiped my face, and dialed the house again. After what seemed like five minutes someone answered. My mom. I sniffed. "Let me speak to dad, please."

"I don't know what to tell you."

Her tone, stiff and cold, hurt.

"Let me just talk to dad. I have to explain it all to him."

"He doesn't want to talk to you."

I've never been so broken in my life, or any time since. By age twenty-two, I'd lost more money than most people will earn in a lifetime. And it wasn't even my money. It was my dad's. Certainly not something to put on a resume. Or a head stone.

With the phone still pressed to my ear, I clicked the receiver button down. I rocked and tried to sort through my thoughts. I lowered the phone into the cradle. I drifted out, past the moon, past the sun, past the Milky Way, spinning slowly through a dozen other galaxies.

All was lost. It was over.

I drifted back from the cosmos and soon felt my bed under me. I stretched out, wailed, and opened the nightstand. I felt around for my mom's .38 Special. I knew it had six rounds in it. I only needed one. I wrapped my fingers around the handle and lifted it onto my lap. The weight surprised me. I lifted the chrome revolver and opened my mouth.

Time for some peace.

Chapter 13
A STILL, SMALL VOICE

C'mon, high roller. Get it done."
I couldn't argue with this voice in my head. I could solve some many of my problems. The shame, the guilt, the torture. I could rest, finally rest. How lovely. I could float away and not have to wake up to that quote machine?

My dad's words thundered in my head, "This is over..."

It was. The weight of blowing the last of my parents' money crushed me. My dad exiling me from his life sentenced me to death. With no dad and no family, I had nothing.

A tear rolled down my cheek and I closed my eyes. I deserved this. I hated myself even more than I hated the damned market. Nine months ago, I looked forward to the life ahead of me. Now I'd give anything to live a boring life in Ponderosa; marry a gorgeous, boring wife, buy a boring ranch house with a boring picket fence; raise boring kids; and live a boring, but peaceful life. All stuff I'd never have in a few seconds when I pulled the trigger.

I thought of my dad again. With no cash reserves, he couldn't even start over. He'd have to take a job somewhere in town, possibly from someone he once outbid at auction. Mom might have to get a job, possibly as a waitress at a diner. Another tear rolled down my face.

My finger tested the action of the trigger. I was about leave behind the months of waking up in a panic, the sickening anxiety in my stomach, the agony of the losses. I'd leave this mess for someone else to clean up unless I could figure how what to do. I raced through my options one last time. I convinced myself nothing would work.

I took one last, deep chest-full of air, held it, and exhaled.

I already missed my family, and Shawn and Justin and Bear. Lack of hope, though, trumps all. "Here goes nothing," I said and started to pull the trigger.

You can pay it back.

What the heck was that? For a moment, I thought someone walked into the room. I looked around. Still alone. Thank goodness. I didn't want someone to witness the mess I was about to make.

You can pay it back. You can work it off. Who else is going to get it back?

This voice. Still and quiet. Unlike anything I'd ever heard. My life had been spent around loud auctioneers, fast-talking businessmen, and loud patrons in a bar.

How much can you earn in a year? You can pay it off in a few. You can work hard. Earn it back.

This voice confused me. I just wanted to escape this mess, escape the hole I'd dug. I tilted the barrel further up at the roof of my mouth and shut my eyes again. I didn't want to miss. Certain of what I wanted to do one second and terrified the next at ending my life, I cried.

I didn't understand why I heard voices. But the voice didn't speak to me from my mind, but rather my heart. That didn't make sense either. Yet, I felt a distant, familiar sense of peace.

What if I devoted every waking hour to working off this debt? What if I worked my butt off? What if I faced each day with an honest determination and went to bed each night confident I'd sleep peacefully because I did the right thing?

My rational mind pushed aside the small voice. *Your dad won't even talk to you. It's over. Hopeless.*

For the first time, I became aware of the evil undertone to these thoughts. Where did they come from? More sinister. I longed for more of the soothing voice.

It returned. *You can earn it back.*

A spark of hope flickered. I sensed real goodness in this voice, goodness I hadn't felt in what seemed liked years. It felt wonderful, wholesome, and tranquil. I soaked in this warmth for a moment, just feeling its presence, its peace, its comfort. Tears came again. This time I welcomed them. I opened my eyes.

The loaded gun rested between my teeth. I took my finger off the trigger and eased the revolver out of my mouth. I laid the gun on the floor. I shivered. What had I almost done?

The gentle voice cooed, smoothing my hurt, guilt, and shame. *Rest now.*

Tears poured down my face. I buried my face in my hands and groaned. "Oh, God." With each sob, the tension eased throughout my body. "My Lord. I will pay it back. I will work so hard, and pay it all back. I swear."

I sobbed until every ounce of stress and anguish left me. The weightlessness returned, but now in a good way. A great way. The burden was gone.

After relaxing in my newfound hope for several minutes, I stood and stretched. The room seemed brighter. The .38 laid on the floor. I picked it up and slammed it back in the drawer, never to tell anyone for years what I almost did.

"I will pay it all back," I muttered, not trying to convince myself but rather proclaimed a creed I'd live by for many, many years.

I couldn't wait to send my parents the first check. It probably wouldn't be much, but in time, I'd return more with each check. I could do this. I could pay back all of it, more than $500,000.

But first, I needed a job. I scanned through the classified section of the newspaper. We didn't have Craigslist or Monster.com back then. I realized I wasn't qualified to do much. That dinged my hope a little. I needed a shot in the arm. I called my dad again.

Mom answered, and after a while dad finally got on the phone, his tone straightforward. No anger. No warmth.

"Dad?" An awkward silence followed. I didn't know what to say once when he spoke to me, but my heart jumped for joy for the first time in a long while. "I'm going to make it all right. I'm going to work until I've paid back every cent." Another moment of silence and then he spoke with a softer tone.

"Well, we've sure got a lot of ground to cover."

"Yeah." I paused. I wouldn't let him take away my hope, but I didn't want to come across as naive either. "I can get a job, finish school and I'll be out in a few months. I should be able to find something decent, and every cent I make over living expenses will go straight to you guys." The pause that followed made me uncomfortable.

"That's appreciated but you have to know there is no money left for school."

I didn't think of that. I guess I was still naive. I wobbled for a second and then focused. "There might be something in the cattle business?"

"You and I both know you don't want to be in the cattle business."

I wondered why that mattered. "I *know* the cattle business."

"I know you do. But I still think A, you're talented in this trading stuff. And B, it's the only way we're going to make the money back."

Not what I wanted to hear. I needed to put the hell and trauma of trading behind me. "I'm just not sure I can keep trading. It's so stressful."

"You need some training. Learn the right way and start small," he said. "That's honestly all we can do, is start small. Then try to grow it back up."

I'd thought of starting small. Dad's comments confirmed my thought. I knew two things—I couldn't make the money I owed my dad any other way than trading, and I still couldn't say no to my dad.

A few days later, I went back to Ponderosa to prepare for Dad's upcoming trial. After meeting with the lawyer, we went back to the house. Since our talk on the phone, I'd found a guy who trained young traders, guys like me who needed help. John Purger in Black Spring, Colorado, owned a brokerage called Independent Trader's Company. He seemed like the perfect mentor for me.

"Do you know if he wants you to work out of his office, or can you work from here?" dad asked.

I'd forgotten to ask that question.

"Don't sweat it." Dad smiled. "You can ask him when you go out there. I guess I'm financing your trip, huh?" He laughed and I put on my best "If you could be so kind" look. He laughed again, handed me a beer, and said "No problem. I'll just add it to your tab."

I half-laughed.

I knew I needed to wait to visit Purger until after the hearings and appeals.

✦

Chapter 14

SOMETHING FINALLY
GOES MY WAY

hree looming court appearances became a distraction. I wanted to focus on what I needed to do to recoup the money, but couldn't. When I put the gun in my mouth, I didn't have hope. Now I did. I felt I'd found a way to make up the money, to return what I lost.

Dad's disorderly conduct charge came up first. We hired the renowned Sonny Stevens, Esquire, a lanky, sixty year-old who sported a thick Magnum, P.I.-style mustache and wore snakeskin boots with his suits. He didn't come cheap and I wasn't sure how my dad paid the fees.

In our first meeting in Stevens' office, he said the goal was to use dad's case to "build credibility for Steve's."

Before we got into the details of the cases, Dad said, "Judge Hollis saw the girl in person. How in the heck are these guys trying to bring a case before him when he wanted to dismiss it? Is there much more we need?"

"Judge Hollis ain't a judge no longer." Stevens raised his eyebrows.

"What?" The word came out loud, much louder than normal from my dad.

"I don't know how our county attorney and his boy managed it, but Judge Hollis has officially retired." Stevens paused, waiting for a response we didn't offer. "Whether willingly or not." He shrugged.

This hurt. A lot. How could we win without Hollis on the bench? The county attorney apparently had more pull than I thought. I was now officially pretty nervous. We found out later the judge's daughter had dated Harris, apparently enough to "force" the judge to retire.

We spent an ungodly amount of time going over details again and again. With Judge Hollis gone, we couldn't afford any mistakes. Eventually we felt like we had a good approach.

Regarding my case, the domestic abuse charges were ludicrous. The pictures of Tammy proved Harris had lied. The criminal mischief concerned me because it was my word against theirs. Stevens wanted a copy of videotape that showed me putting a Dixie cup over the lens and not destroying the camera. The fact the Dixie cup covered the lens worried Sonny. Depending on how much the cup covered, Harris could have gone in undetected and smashed the camera without anyone seeing him. If we could show the domestic abuse charges were a lie, and the prosecution couldn't produce video of me destroying the camera, we should be in good shape.

During the trip to town, I also discovered many of the townsfolk, the same ones who had cheered on my athletic endeavors a few years before, seemed to have turned on me. At a diner, with the place pretty full, I saw familiar faces, smiled and nodded in greeting. A couple at one table averted my eyes.

What the heck? What was their deal?

A waitress who had been there for years called out from the counter, "Just seat yourself anywhere, sir."

Sir? What the heck was going on? Usually it was "Hey Steve, how are you doing honey?" Everyone knew me around here. This was weird.

I passed a few more familiar faces that ignored me. I wasn't being paranoid. After I noticed a woman whispering to her husband and stop when I looked their way, I called Shawn.

"You know Ponderosa man," he said. "That cop has been running his mouth to anyone who will listen. I'm sure half the town acts like they witnessed you beating Tammy firsthand."

I shook my head. I knew it before I asked, but I had to hear it from someone else. Small town gossipers with nothing better to do. At twenty-three, life was getting pretty darn complicated for a kid who just wanted to do the right thing.

We met Sonny at the courthouse on a Monday morning for my dad's trial. I had major butterflies, but Dad looked like he was about to get into a boxing ring. We stepped into the courtroom where we were to battle Harris and his buddy.

After the typical preliminaries of "All rise", etc., the county attorney went first. He peacocked and paraded, dramatized and exaggerated. Harris predictably spewed lies. After an infuriating hour or so, the prosecution rested.

Then Sonny took over. He first presented eight local cases in which Harris had overstepped his bounds to the point of breaking the law. Sonny put into evidence a number of affidavits, and even called some witnesses from other cases, to prove Harris and the county attorney had drummed up cases. The county attorney cried "Relevance?" but he was shot down by the new judge.

Dad took the stand and I was proud of how he handled himself. He could get testy at times, particularly when someone tried to screw him over. That day, he kept his cool and answered every question in a calm manner.

The jury found my dad innocent. I looked over at Harris. He snorted. Too bad, I thought. I told you that you messed with the wrong person. Grinning, I high-fived Dad and Sonny. Now I had hope for my case in a couple of weeks.

When I returned to Ponderosa for my trial, I stopped at the local bookstore to pick up the March edition of *Futures Magazine*. First, I glanced at *Glacier Gazette* and did a double take. I thought I might be hallucinating. The top headline screamed lies about me and my family.

I couldn't move. I thought I might hyperventilate. Before I blew the proverbial gasket, I grabbed a paper, paid for it, and left. I wondered if I'd ever catch a break.

I went to my parents' home where I read the poorly written article. The writer put in details that made me wonder where they got the information. Hyped-up information from the police report certainly left the reader ready to convict the "suspect" who "allegedly" broke his girlfriend's nose after recklessly squandering a small fortune of his parent's money on the markets without authorization.

This felt like yet another straw that might break me. Through all this mess, I had been able to remain positive. I didn't know how much more I could take. Anger, then guilt, then sadness took turns pounding at my heart.

I wondered if I should bother with this fight anymore. Why even fight to do the right thing when life keeps kicking you in the face? I was just trying to stop Tammy from driving drunk with her own daughter in the car. Look what I got for it. I was trying to help my dad get his money back and got sucked into that black hole without any help. Why bother?

The only thing stronger than the depression was my resolve to prove everyone wrong. Determined more than ever to expose Harris and his corrupt attorney, I clipped the article and put it in a binder.

In the weeks leading up to my trial, I prepped religiously for my trial, asking Sonny the same questions over and over, and drilling every scenario into Tammy. The morning, I don't remember which day of the week, of the trial, despite the confidence gained from my dad's verdict, I was nervous because the county attorney had requested a jury trial. This meant the judge, who saw through the lies the first time wouldn't decide my fate, a jury of my peers held that honor.

Harris and the county attorney did their best to paint me as a monster who enjoyed beating up his girlfriend. To do this, they worked Tammy over pretty good on the stand in an effort to make it appear as though she was a terrified, battered girlfriend who was lying because of Stockholm syndrome. The county attorney managed to confuse her on some issues and it did appear as though she could be lying to protect me.

But Sonny saved the day with this examination of the dispatcher who was on duty the night of my arrest. He started with the typical questions: "When did your shift begin? How long were you on duty? When did you leave? Did you see Mr. Meyers being brought into the jail? Did you know he placed the Dixie cup over the camera lens?"

Sonny waited until the end to ask his biggest question. "What did you witness after Mr. Meyers was released on bail?"

The dispatcher peered over at Harris with a look filled with contempt. It appeared the department was tired of dealing with him too.

"I observed Officer Harris go into the cell, take the Dixie cup off the observation camera and dismantle it, leaving it hanging out by its wires. He then took pictures of the dismantled camera and included them in the report."

A gasp echoed through the courtroom.

"You mean to tell me that an officer of the law deliberately falsified evidence to convict an innocent man?" Sonny said.

"I'm just telling you what I observed."

"Officer, is there a copy of the tape, from that night?"

"There is, and it shows Mr. Meyers placing the Dixie cup over the lens. It stops recording right before he is released on bail."

"Oh it does?" Sonny turned to the jury with a thoughtful finger on his mouth. "Is that typical procedure? I mean to stop the recording before the victim is released?"

I caught the word victim dropped in there and smiled.

"No sir," the dispatcher said. "Typically the tape runs the entire night."

That was all Sonny needed. Harris squirmed during Sonny's closing arguments. I loved that, watching Harris lose his arrogance. I, on the other hand, was furious. It is difficult to explain how sickening it is to hear someone blatantly lie about you in court. And lie about charges that could send you to prison for years. Harris was a creep without a badge, which made him an outright public menace with one.

The daylong trial took a lot out of me—the swings in emotion from anger to content to fear to hope was grueling. But the end, I thought I wanted to give up on life again.

After a brutal day of hearing questionable testimony, the jury took about ninety minutes to decide my fate. I sat as unemotional as I could while the jury filed back into the box. I don't think I breathed when the officer took the verdict from the jury foreman, gave it to the judge, and returned it to her. She told and said in a clear tone, "Regarding the charges of domestic abuse and criminal mischief ... the jury finds the defendant innocent."

I almost jumped up and shouted. Sonny discretely held up his hand. The look on his face concerned me. More charges. My heart sank.

"Regarding the counts of disorderly conduct and resisting arrest ... the jury finds the defendant ... guilty."

"What?" I looked over at Sonny and he shook his head.

I glanced at Harris. He smirked. I wanted to punch him.

We left the courtroom and Sonny spoke first. "Don't sweat it. We'll file an appeal. This is good news. You're not going to jail, and that my friend, is a victory."

"But they heard Tammy's testimony. They saw this guy has a history of lying?" I was still pretty worked up. This all felt wrong.

"I guess the jury figured where there's smoke, there must be a fire. It's certainly not the first time that's happened." He gave me a weak smile that said I'm sorry pal. "We'll file an appeal."

Sonny filed an appeal and we got a hearing a month later. There was no way I was going to let them get away with finding me guilty of even those minor charges. I wanted the town of Ponderosa to thank me for getting Harris off the street.

At the hearing, Sonny pointed out Harris' word couldn't be trusted, that Harris had lied about me beating Tammy and smashing the camera. Sonny also reiterated my dad's charge of disorderly conduct had been thrown out by the judge.

We won the appeal. All charges were dismissed. After much discussion with my attorney, I decided to file a lawsuit against the city.

Instead of a much-need vacation, I decompressed for a couple of weeks. This allowed me to finalize my preparations for the meeting with Purger the following month. I looked forward to getting away from Wyoming for a while and leave behind the whispers, averted looks, and skewed newspaper reports.

Although I hoped to do some sightseeing and visit with my aunt and uncle in Black Spring, I focused on the meeting. I could not screw this up.

I met Purger, a much younger man than I envisioned, in his office, located in an attractive, modern complex. Although five-foot-nine, well-groomed with dark hair, he owned the room. His herringbone suit bellowed "Ivy League alumni." Purger gave me a quick tour of the office, much different than the livestock casino of my first experience. We picked up his wife Jill and ate a great new French restaurant in town. After lunch of Chardonnay and foie gras, Purger asked about my trading experience. With two failed experiences, I'm sure I didn't impress him with my expertise. Still, he wanted to know if I planned to open an office in Wyoming.

"Well, I'm not really sure I'm ready for that." I wanted to learn the right way this time. "I'm probably more interested in working out here in Black Spring, with you."

He seemed to like the idea. "Is there any business you might be able to bring over?"

I didn't have much—some close friends and family—but that didn't seem to bother him.

Purger explained I needed to get a license and a $15,000 good faith deposit— to reduce his liability—before he could hire me. Fifteen thousand was a lot of money. In return, I'd receive an office and access to his six-person office staff. He planned to take "a slightly higher commission" than if I ran my own office.

All this sounded good to me. Purger had a lot of what I wanted—beautiful office, lovely home with Eden-like landscaping, and a wife who made heads turn. More importantly, I wanted this time to learn and do things the right way from the start. I figured it was a good fit, mainly because I hadn't checked out other brokerage jobs. And the truth was that time was not on my side. I needed to make something happen... and fast.

Chapter 15
Yet Another Mistake

I looked forward to working for Independent Trader's Company. John Purger seemed to have it all together—a huge house, beautiful wife, people scurrying around him all the time. Pretty heady stuff for a guy my age with a goal and a dream. I thought working for ITC would fix all I'd messed up.

Although Purger took a small cut for commission, I had full use all of his research staff and back office gear. Best of all, and this was the clincher for me, Purger mentored me. I not only wanted that, I needed a mentor.

The one downside, a biggie, was the $15,000 for a "good faith deposit." I didn't have the money and I felt certain Dad didn't either. I shared all this with my dad in a conversation.

After a long silence, he said, "That's about all I have left to invest for you. Even that will put me in a bit of a pinch."

In moments like this, I realized the depth of my dad's endless love. I bit back the emotions and said, in a more choky voice than I intended, "I'll make it up to you. I'm going to work and study so hard."

"I know you will pal," he said. Again, my dad's belief in me. Unflappable and unending.

That evening I ordered a home study kit for my Series Three commodities license. I endured mixed emotions about trading again—the weirdness of getting back in after swearing I would never again offset by the sense of dealing with unfinished business. I hated being beaten, and the opportunity to learn to trade, and actually make money, brought a certain satisfaction with it. I made a silent vow to master the art. I slowly got excited about the opportunity. A few weeks later, I drove to Rapid City, South Dakota, and passed the test without breaking a sweat.

Time to make some money.

During the three-week it takes to receive the license after passing the test, I talked with Tammy about moving to Black Spring. Her response surprised me. I wouldn't have been heartbroken if she wanted to stay behind, but she wanted to go. I didn't argue with her. She stood by me while losing the money and the trial. I couldn't dump her at this point.

We agreed I'd move first and she'd follow in a few weeks to look for a job. If she found one, she and Tabitha would join me. Even though I was mentally committed to her, the scenario seemed just about perfect because I could be away from her for good stretches.

I looked forward to a fresh start. I craved the energy of John Purger's office. While I waited for my license, I packed for the move. In between, I talked with potential clients. Bear and his brother said they had my back and promised to get some money together and open an account. My sister Madison and her husband, Bob, a major supporter during this rough time, agreed to open an account. Reggie also sounded interested. The future began to look a little brighter.

During this two-week span of waiting and packing, I realized I broke a promise to God. During the Bill Black debacle, I said I'd live the right way when the account got back in the black. I reneged, taking control of my life and doing things without the Lord's guidance. Worse, I had yet to repent for not keeping my word.

I wondered if that promise still mattered because the whole bottom fell out anyway. I mulled over that thought. I could've gotten out ahead, but chose not to. God held up His end of the bargain. But I kind of shrugged it off and thanked God for the opportunity with Purger. The last thing I wanted was a guilty conscious when things finally looked they may turn around in my favor. This time, although I'd eventually be living with Tammy again, I promised to not party as much when I got up there. I'd focus on work instead.

My first day at Independent Trader's Company was beyond what I imagined. Purger cruised around the office and responded to questions instantly, as though he had been anticipating them for hours. He worked hard. Not to be outdone, I took my list of potential clients and made calls to build my client list.

Bob and Madison were ready to roll and opened an account right away. Jay Michaels, a good friend, opened an account. So did Reggie. Bear and his brother showed their support by taking out a $10,000 loan for a "boat." The banker didn't even ask to see the boat. He only said, "Sounds nice," and handed over the cashier's check. That wasn't enough for Bear, though. He recruited some farmers from his area.

John seemed impressed with my resolve. A couple of brokers in the office next to me taught me a ton about technical details. Between trades, I hit the phones as hard as I could in an effort to land cattle hedgers. I knew I'd need time to land some big accounts, but for the moment I wasn't about to starve. I also studied books and charts. For the first time I wasn't a real greenhorn. The more I learned however, the more horrified and distraught I became over my experience with Black. A broker should never, ever have allowed trading like that, let alone encourage it.

For the first few months, Tammy and I met at a halfway point about every other weekend. The absence made me miss her. Our trips ended when she found a good job working as part of the hospitality team at the Marriot in town. I genuinely enjoyed Tammy when she and Tabitha first moved in, but after a few weeks I spent more and more time at work. I had a goal and the only way to achieve it, in my mind, was to work harder and longer.

Three months later, around fall, it seemed the roller coaster was about to level off. Until I listened to office chatter that I'd ignored for months. I heard a few rumblings of discontent and learned about Purger's unethical trading practices. I put my head on my desk and sighed. I won't go into detail for fear of giving someone an idea of how to commit fraud. After this discovery, I knew I couldn't work for Purger. And I wondered if there were any honest people in this business.

I heard some of the other brokers whispering about getting out as well. Some of the brokers were a little older so it hit them harder. Getting out and starting over might be difficult for them. Some decided to tough it out. Some decided to make contingency plans. I was among that group.

I gritted my teeth however when I thought of my $15,000. I'd strangle Purger if he as much as tried to think of screwing me out of the money. In that moment, I realized I now disliked Purger after being enamored by him just a few months ago.

Monday, October 19, 1987, the Dow Jones Index Average dropped 508 points, more than 22-percent in one day. The dive in what became known as Black Monday began in Hong Kong, made its way to Europe, and finally hit Wall Street.

All of my clients and I were trading in long cattle positions. We could take a hit, a big hit. When the market crashes, liquidity dries up. And we were worried the economy might slow down beef consumption. The futures markets closed limit down, which means you can't get out of your positions, four days in a row, and I flashbacked to the previous summer. We were losing a ton of money. The sickening anxiety, the despair returned. The brokers at the office all said they'd never seen anything like this before, and their business would never be the same.

Those four days were some of the longest of my life. Not only did I have family money tied up, I now had friend's money too. When the market is limit down, it's locked. You can't trade. You watch, and hope, your accounts don't slip far enough that you never recover.

The market turned and recovered—a little. I knew enough by now to hold my long positions and wait for the market to climb a bit. When the market leveled off, I salvaged some of the some of the losses but was back in a hole again. I couldn't believe it. I called my clients, many of whom reassured me I wasn't at fault. I still felt terrible because most of them traded to help me out.

While watching, I decided to leave Independent Trader's Company. I planned to tell Purger on Friday. Feeling like a beaten man, I drug myself to work and tried to stay calm until a meeting around 3:00 p.m. A few of us, Purger included, gathered in a conference room. I broke the chit chat with an announcement. "John, I'm giving my notice today."

He didn't object, a good indication he knew that I knew.

"If you could write me a check for my $15,000 deposit," I said, feeling relieved and bold, "I'll make sure all my accounts are wrapped up in good order, and all loose ends tied up."

"I can accept your resignation," he began, smirking, "but you will not see your deposit for two years pal."

I smiled, clenched my jaw, and looked down at the table sideways. "Don't even mess with me. I'm not the kind of chump to take that sort of crap lying down."

"It's law. Clients have a two-year period to come back on a broker so we have to wait to make sure you've been handling everything with our client's accounts above board. We have to make sure no disputes come up."

The "our" part made me see red. "You know I need the money. And more than that, you know I have zero problems with my accounts. I want my money. Now."

"Two years and it's yours."

He grinned and I snapped. I lunged across the table and grabbed for his lapels. He jolted backward. And shrieked like a little girl. He stumbled into the corner, screaming now for help. I got my hands on him for just a moment before two of his guards tackled and restrained me. I wrestled free, but they stood between me and Purger, who seemed visibly shaken.

I hoped my attack scared him enough into cutting the check. It wasn't. He kept the money, as well as an additional $7,000 in commissions due to me.

I didn't worry about Purger pressing charges. If he did, I'd spill the beans on every, greasy, dirty little secret about him and ITC that I knew.

I'd been hustled again. And forced to start over. Again. How many times would I travel down this road?

Despite the crushing feeling of losing the principle in the big crash, I knew I must get back to making money or I'd never be able to repay my friends—or my dad. I really could use the $22,000 Purger owed, but I knew I'd never see the money.

Tom Golovkin, a good kid from Nebraska who wanted to get some experience outside of his dad's firm, left a couple of messages on my answering machine at home. One was pretty funny. He said the disgruntled at ITC revered me for my Incredible Hulk impersonation. More importantly, he wanted to have lunch and discuss opening a branch office for his dad in Black Spring. We met and worked out the details. I called my clients and notified them I'd left ITC. I danced carefully around slander laws about Purger being a thief, and I told them about the branch office in Black Spring. Every one of my clients moved with me. The entire process took about a month and soon I was back making trades again.

The effects of the crash lasted a while. The market didn't snap back like many hoped and prayed. I focused on landing new business. I learned I wasn't a bad salesman and inherently understood the social side of trading. All things being equal, if they like you, they'll stick with it through a few bumps. All things not being equal, they'll still stick with you.

More importantly, I learned God still took care of me, even in another dark hour.

Chapter 16
A TURN IN MY FAVOR

ld Chicago's, a great restaurant, sat across the street from the Marriot where Tammy worked. We dined there often and enjoyed the interesting mix of yuppies and white collar professionals. Most went to network. One Saturday for lunch we chose to sit at the bar because of the long wait for a table. That decision changed my fortunes—you could say, my luck with trading.

I sat next to a silver-haired gentleman with a thick, English accent who pounded beers like they were sodas. The female bartender seemed to laugh at most of his jokes, so I eavesdropped on a few.

"So a blonde, feeling pretty confident in her handywoman skills, decided to canvass a wealthy neighborhood." He paused to take a sip of beer, knowing just about everyone within earshot was listening. "She went to the front door of the first house and asked the owner if he had any jobs for her. 'Well, my porch does need painting,' he replied. 'What would you charge for a job like that?' Thinking a little too hard about it, she answered, 'How about fifty dollars?'" The bartender chuckled and a wicked twinkle shone in the Englishman's eye.

"The man agreed and told her he already had the paint and brushes in the garage. The blonde set off to go and begin her task. The man's wife, having heard the conversation asked, 'Does that wee lass know the porch wraps around the house?' The man nodded, 'She rightly should. She was standing on it.' Twenty minutes later, the blonde knocks on the door, to collect her money. 'Bloody, hell. You're finished already?' the owner exclaimed. 'Oh yes,' said the blonde, 'and I even had paint left over. So I gave it two coats.'

"'Well, I'll be a sheared sheep herder,' the man shouted, obviously impressed, and reached into his pocket for the $50."

"'Oh and by the way,' the blonde added, 'that's not a Porch... it's a bloody Ferrari.'"

His delivery doubled the rest of us over in laughter. The Englishman, clearly proud of himself, turned to me, and nodded as if to say you liked that, didn't you?

"You are a riot," I said, still laughing. "The name's Steve Meyers." I extended my hand. "Please, let me buy you a drink."

"Jim Porter, old chap," he said, shaking my hand. "Cheers mate," he added, clinking my frosty mug with his beer. "I'll take that drink, and you can tell me what fascinating things you do for a living." I nodded to the bartender and she poured him a fresh brew.

"I'm a futures broker," I said, not wanting to sound desperate.

"A successful one?" Porter eyed me up and down, looking for rich details he may have missed before.

"Most would say." I smiled.

He laughed and clinked my glass again. "I like that, mate. But I'm afraid I don't know much about futures. Please enlighten a curious old codger."

I explained cattle loads, breeding times of the year, feeder cattle and all the enthralling things of the cattle trading universe. He appeared fascinated. I wondered what he did for a living. He dressed casually, but his shoes looked like ostrich-skin.

"So how did you get into *that*?"

"I was raised by a cattle trading son of a cattle trader," I said. "My dad began dabbling in futures, and I took over."

"So you have a lifetime of inside info, do you?"

His interest piqued my interest into the questions. "Well, it helps to a degree. But yes, it definitely gives me an edge."

"I'm an engineer," he said.

I nodded and racked my brain to think of all the possible avenues of engineering I could think of. "Civil, mechanical, electrical?"

"Chemical."

"Interesting. As in industrial chemicals?" I could have kicked myself. I didn't sound very informed.

"Yes." He tipped his head. I breathed a sigh of relief, and let him talk. "Nuclear applications more specifically."

Intrigued, I said, "Tell me more."

"Actually I have patented a device, and a chemical process that greatly improves the efficiency of extracting uranium."

My eyes widened. "Uranium? No kidding."

"I'm quite proud of it."

"Isn't uranium mined though?" I remembered reading a little about it after the Chernobyl incident.

"Yes, but mining is quite expensive," he said. "In many applications, my device and chemical process is a far more elegant and lucrative option." I nodded for him to go on, but Tammy squirmed and cleared her throat. Shame on me for not introducing her earlier. I made the introduction and took part in some small talk with the two of them before getting back to the serious discussion with Porter.

He explained the basic mechanics of his device and chemical process. Instead of mining uranium ore, he'd inject a chemical solution into a series of wells at a site. The solution would leech the uranium, along with a few other valuable minerals, into recovery wells, and his devices then would pump the uranium-rich solution to a plant. His device performed a large part of refinement called ion-exchange that extracted only the uranium. The result, known as yellow cake, created a raw form of uranium, ready for conversion at a nuclear facility.

Not sure if he loved his job or because of my fascination with him, I found the entire description of great interest. Even Tammy managed to focus for a few minutes. He explained for a good while, and then we chatted more about various topics. I noticed how easily we played off each other. The people around us must have thought we were long-time friends, as he set up a witty statement and I knocked it out of the park.

When he stood to leave, after a dozen beers or so, I gave him my card and told him I hoped to see him again.

"You will," he said with a genuine smile.

Five days later, on Thursday, my office phone rang. Porter's brogue on the other end put a smile on my face. He said he wanted to meet right away. My smile widened.

"For you good sir, I'm free all day,"

He chuckled and came to my office. He wanted to know more about trading and the prospects of making money. I sold him on the potential for huge gains without minimizing the risk.

"I'm in." He nodded. "I'm going to write you a check to open an account and I want you to be aggressive."

I liked his style. "How aggressive?"

"Here's five thousand dollars. Don't worry about losing it." He scribbled out the check and handed it to me.

"I'll see you a week from Monday, old boy." He smiled and left.

I liked that he took risks. I needed someone like him right now. Something about him made me feel this account could become something good. And it did.

I reminded myself to remain patient and disciplined, but above all calm. I obsessed over my charts for the next few hours and sure enough, I spotted what I believed to be an opportunity approaching in the cattle market. It appeared the market was primed to sell off. So I planned to sell—go short—on Porter's behalf. If my estimations were correct, we were set to net some outstanding profit. It would, however, take pristine timing. I decided to wait until Monday.

Monday, I reviewed the charts and considered the trades again. The market appeared head for a downturn. I sold five cattle, which used up Porter's margin money. But at the very least, I wanted to show Porter a solid percentage gain. The selloff began the next day and continued through the rest of the week. The account went through the roof. I wished he'd given $50,000, but we still made money on the $5,000. At market close on Friday, a nice amount of money sat in Porter's account. I couldn't wait to see his face when I told him.

Porter came to the office Monday morning. I showed him the profit we made.

"Bloody hell, mate. You doubled it."

I smiled and nodded, like this kind of thing happened every day for my clients.

"This is what you can do?"

"This was a pretty decent run." I chuckled and tried to temper his enthusiasm a little. "I've had some downs in the midst of my ups, but yeah..."

"Get your jacket," he said. "We're going to lunch."

We ended up at Pier 41, a San Francisco-inspired seafood place with a great bar and friendly patrons. I'd been here a few times. Good seafood, lots of beers on draft, friendly wait staff, and lots of nets, fishing poles, signs, and fake fish on the walls.

We sat at a table in the back. Porter dove right in with, "I want to form a partnership with you."

I loved his direct approach, but he surprised me. I raised my eyebrows.

"Hear me out," he said. "I have contacts around the world from England to South Africa to Australia, from all my business travels. All these guys are players in the markets, and I know we could get five million dollars right now, and way more depending on how you do. We can form a company and split everything fifty-fifty. You trade and I'll secure the money."

The waitress interrupted with scaloppini bruschetta.

Porter suggested I take one. I took a bite, and savored the taste for a moment. "I'm flattered by your proposal. Sounds very interesting, but I have a pretty solid clientele right now."

"Do you have at least ten millionaires and a couple of billionaires thrown in for good measure?" He knew how to up the ante. I tried my best to keep my poker face while he continued. "Dump your investors and we'll start fresh. If this will take a little time, I'll pay all your monthly expenses until we get up and running."

This sounded too good to be true. I didn't want to lump Porter in with Bill Black and John Purger. But this seemed much like those experiences—just what I wanted and needed to hear at the beginning, only to fall apart soon after.

"There is something you should know about me."

I told him everything. Bill Black. The dairy buyout. Chernobyl. The commodities disaster. How I'd lost everything my parents had. I even told him about the arrest. The whole world knew my story anyway.

Jim stood, and for a second I wondered if he was about to say, "Thanks but no thanks" and leave. Instead he sat next to me in the booth, put his arm around me, and looked me in the eye. "Bloody hell, Steve. You've been through a lot." I appreciated his gesture. "I'm going to make you a millionaire. You'll be able to pay your parents back in no time. What is done is done. Let's just move forward."

A break. What I'd been waiting for. I struggled to hide my excitement. I thought of Bear, his brother, and my other clients. I knew some stuck it out after the crash because of our personal relationship. I exhaled, held out my hand, and shook his as tight as I could. "You've got yourself a deal ... mate."

Chapter 17

FRESH START

I needed a week to close my business. Perhaps the toughest call was to Bear and his brother. Man, I loved those guys. I wanted to make them some money, but the unstable market prevented that. We endured a rough six months to just break even. I called them first, and it seemed they were happy to get out. After them, I spoke with the rest of my clients. No one complained about me shutting the doors.

I told my dad I felt good about this new endeavor with Jim. "Well," Dad said, "you do have a million-dollar personality, and I've always said it is going to take you places. Remember what I've told you since you were a little boy, you can do anything you put your mind to." His words took me from Cloud Nine to Cloud Ten.

While closing my office, Jim and I met frequently. During one of the first meetings, Jim offered a company vehicle and monthly allowance of $1,500 until things got rolling. That money covered rent and groceries. Not bad for a startup. And more stability than I experienced in a long time.

As for the legalities, Jim suggested we incorporate as partners, and split all profits fifty-fifty. I liked this guy. Seemed fair. For the name, we decided on Wise International Investments.

I also needed a clearing broker to run my trades through, and hopefully give me access to a quote system. I preferred someone local with the hope of leveraging the potential of large clients for some office space. I called Jim Howitzer, from the futures circles, a smaller, more honest John Purger. Jim bit right away on the uranium players, and he offered me a private office with the desired access to quotes. In return, I'd run all my trades through him.

Although Jim and I accomplished a lot in the meetings, it felt more like hanging out. Jim's wit was sharp as an industrial diamond. We bounced off each other to the point where people wanted to sit near us when we were out. This was fun, something I hadn't had in quite some time.

After the first month Tammy needled me when the money didn't roll in. I told her a multi-million deal in Australia was in the works. That wasn't an outright lie. A major client of Jim's expressed interest in the American futures market, which is much, much bigger than the market in Australia.

Two months later, I still hadn't reeled in my big fish. I still needed the monthly allowance from Jim to pay bills. Near the end of the year, I stopped by his house to pick up my check. His wife Estelle, a plump lady with cropped, graying hair, answered the door and gave me the check while pursing her lips. I asked her if something was wrong.

"Money is a little tight right now," she said, "so I'm a little stressed."

A little taken aback, all I could manage was a quick, "Oh."

"How is it going generating some business?"

"Jim has the leads. Whenever he introduces me to a contact, I'm working hard on the close."

Estelle nodded, obviously not impressed with the lack of clients so far.

"There's huge potential here," I said. "We're going to nail it."

"That'd be wonderful. Let's hope sooner, rather than later."

I didn't expect that response. A familiar stab of anxiety twisted in my gut. I brooded the rest of the day. Eventually I reached the conclusion that, although I really was feeling more secure, after three months with not one of Jim's contacts opening an account, things were too tight for comfort.

Since he asked me to join him, I wondered why Jim wanted me to drop my existing clientele. I assumed he wanted me to focus 100-percent on our venture. I did, but we weren't closing anything. And not for a lack of trying. Jim would do the elevator pitch, get them to agree to a meeting with me, sometimes by phone. I knocked it out of the park every time by getting the potential clients excited about the futures game.

So, why couldn't I close a single deal? Maybe because of my track record. These guys weren't fools by any means. My doubling of Jim's meager $5,000 and a great sales pitch just might not be enough to get the investors to fork over a million bucks.

This venture did not take off as quickly as I hoped, and my parents suffered some more because of it. I realized two great salesmen could generate a lot of hype in their midst, and unfortunately gloss over some of the glaring pitfalls. My patience ran thin at this point and I'd grown tired of living on potential.

I called Jim, who was out of town on business. "While we're working on getting some big fish," I said, "don't you think it'd make sense if I started trading my own retail accounts again, just take the pressure off a bit? This will give us time to work on the bigger game plan?"

Jim remained silent for a few seconds, his way of absorbing the information. "Is it tight for you? Financially?"

"It's fine. I really do appreciate you covering my expenses while we get this thing off the ground. It's just I need to start making a plan to send some money back to my parents."

"I suppose it is taking a little longer than we hoped," Jim said. "I do still believe there is tremendous potential there."

"As do I. None of that will change."

"Do you think having other accounts might distract you from our work when something breaks for us?"

"I'll make sure it doesn't," I said.

Later in the conversation, Jim mentioned one of his buddies, Colin, thought I should spend some time in Australia after the first of year. I liked the idea.

I'd always wanted to go to Sydney, where Colin lived. In high school, I put up posters of the Sydney Opera House and the bridge on my bedroom wall.

"I'd be over the moon if I can make the trip," I said.

"Not if," he chided, "when."

The next day, I went down to Nick's office. After a brief meeting with him, we chatted with the four other brokers in his firm. I instantly liked these guys when I met them the first time, and we started up right where we left. Within minutes we were laughing hysterically and bragging about the jets and Lamborghinis we'd buy. This felt right to me. I looked forward to pounding the pavement again, and reeling in some of my own business.

These guys offered a few great ideas on where to begin generating leads. The ace in the hole was Nick's son, Nick Jr., a runner in what we called the meat pit, or trading floor. He heard all the scoop first and happily provided us with the inside knowledge.

I called every connection I knew, hit my custom generated lead-list hard, and pretty soon the clients were rolling in again. Every time I considered taking a breather, I thought back to the pursed lips of Jim's wife and how she begrudgingly handed me the check.

I beat the streets and milked every contact. Within a few months, I built a decent clientele list. With the help of my buddies at the office, the extra income trickled in, but not enough to start paying back my parents. With two irons in the fire, and Jim paying my allowance, I knew things would take off at some point.

I continued trading through most of 1989. Between my skills and knowledge being honed again by my pals at Nick's firm, I was back in my element. Tammy and I still struggled, and she liked to remind me when the money trickled in, we were still far from easy street.

Jim became more aggressive in lining up potential clients with deep pockets. Several interested parties still hung on the hook, but we could not get these guys to commit. I never struggled with that in the past.

I knew from my other trades, I could make these guys real money if one—just one—showed a little faith. As with most ventures, landing the first client gave other potential clients confidence to sign on.

Around the middle of the year, I sat down with Jim and discussed a plan I'd been mulling over. I proposed we represent other money managers, raise money for them, and take a cut. The key was to find managers with good, long track records, whose earning we could represent as part of our "group." I hoped to lure big-money investors into the futures arena. This also would help me build my record as well. Jim loved the idea.

After some thought, I wanted to take it a step even further. I called up several managers of successful money managers and proposed my futures plan. These contacts managed a stable of money managers specializing in various trading areas, and investors could pick and choose, and diversify with traders across the group. It's best to give options to investors.

This plan allowed me to present an array of successful investors to our prime clients, match them up to investors who specialized in their interest, and show them the best track records. This hooked them, and by October 1989, we were ready to execute the plan.

I also received great personal news that month. Jim called one day and asked right off, "Would you happen to have a decent luggage set?"

I did, and then Jim explained Colin wanted me in Australia after the first of the year. I'd given up on make the trip. "This is absolutely awesome. Are there any potential clients lined up?"

"No, mate. Colin has leads, but I'm fronting my hard-earned money so you can go and do more than lounge at the beaches. You'll be knocking on doors. I've given very specific instructions to Colin to ensure you stay away from every bar and go to church three times a week."

I laughed, and a few weeks later I landed at Kingford Smith International Airport at 5:30 a.m. on a warm Monday morning. By the time we landed, I'd been up for nearly twenty-four hours, sat next to a guy who was airsick the entire twelve-hour flight from Los Angeles, but here I was, in Sydney. A place I'd dreamed of visiting. I collected my bags and walked out of the international arrivals gate to see a tall, distinguished gentleman with a huge smile on his face. Colin.

I spent my first day in Oz walking to the wrong side of the car for the passenger's seat, mixing up some of the local lingo, meeting Colin's wife Jessica and his two children, Layla and David, and enjoying a dip in their pool.

I lay my head back and looked up at the perfect blue sky with fluffy clouds. I closed my eyes for a few seconds and thought how great this all was. I knew my big break loomed right around the corner. I'd charm the Australian dollars out of these investors by the millions. I'd fly home and flaunt my success to Tammy. Then I drifted off to sleep.

When I awoke, the sun sat halfway down the horizon. I rubbed my face. Dang, that hurt. I looked down at my body. Bright red. And much warmer that it should be. I touched my arms. They hurt too. Great, sunburn. But even with a sunburn, I'd take a hot, summer day over a snowy, fall day in Colorado.

I spent a total of three weeks in Australia, mostly working, but also enjoyed a few sights, some unexpected. One of my best moments was the morning I saw the Sydney Opera House. Jessica took me to the city and suggested we take the ferry instead of the regular road route. Coming from the Midwest, I'd never been on a ferry. Near the end of the ferry ride, Jessica said, almost yelling, "It's time."

"For what?"

She just motioned with her hand and walked to the front of the ferry. "Just watch as we turn the bend."

As if appearing out of nowhere, the Sydney Opera House, with its unique half moon peaks, came into view. Years of longing and wanting crashed over me. I thought of the many nights I stared at the poster of this majestic building. Now, I stood—mouth agape at the most spectacular view of the Opera House possible.

I tried to hide the tears but Jessica put her arm around me. "This is my favorite landmark to show friends. Isn't that bridge and Opera House just magnificent?"

"You don't understand. This has been a dream of mine since high school." I sniffled and wiped away tears. "I honestly can't thank you enough."

Jessica smiled and took pictures for me, letting me soak in this special moment.

At that time, the managed futures sector was still in its infancy and far from a billion dollar industry. I knew futures, though, and knew I could convince some Aussies to invest. Full of testosterone-fueled confidence, I made numerous calls to Colin's contacts. My accent helped to get my foot in the door.

Early during the first week of my visit, Colin dropped me off downtown at the Sydney Futures Exchange. At first it seemed a lame "guided tour" sort of thing. Tired of the person droning on, I asked to meet some of the officials. I worked the old Wyoming charm and soon I sat down to lunch with two middle-aged big bosses. They genuinely seemed interested in what I talked about, and expressed their desire in promoting their own markets in the U.S. I constructed a little impromptu game plan and pitched the idea that some of my managers could potentially incorporate their markets into our trading. They loved it and once I dangled that carrot, the information flowed like a river. I arranged to meet them again in the morning if they could bring some of their local traders to meet.

Colin dropped me off again, and my new friends introduced me to a few local guys who traded their own account on the floor. We went to lunch again and had a great conversation discussing our best and worst trades. I won hands down on the worst trade story. They all seemed rather sympathetic towards me after recounting the Bill Black Commodities debacle, and proceeded to give me even more information and advice on the local markets, including some must-see traders who were the main players.

One day while out with Colin and Jessica, I struck up a conversation with the rugged locals whom I discovered were mostly cattle ranchers who referred to their ranches as stations. I talked shop with them, and soon a crowd gathered, fascinated at the Yank in the city attire. I loved Australia and felt more at home with my "tribe."

The following week I met more than a dozen CFOs, and the following week even more. I put on my "Class 1, Grade A" charm, and left everything on the table in those board rooms. Each meeting went pretty much the same. I met with three or four of the company's top brass. I gave a brief history of the managed futures industry, and talked about the negative correlation my traders had with the equity markets. "In other words," I said, "investors can jump on this opportunity to diversify and reduce risk, while still ensuring strong gains." Most of the executives were very interested. Like back in the U.S., each company wanted someone else to commit first. Again, I needed just one person to bite. No one did.

When the big 'ole jetliner took off the U.S., I'd accomplished some personal goals of seeing the opera house and harbor. More importantly, I'd made some headway into making money for our business.

Chapter 18

HOPE SPRINGS ETERNAL

I loved Australia, the culture, the industry, the people. I returned with a long list of contacts and great memories. But more importantly—hope. If I could break into that market, and spend the rest of my days in Sydney, I wouldn't even hesitate. I wasn't sure about the future of my relationship with Tammy if I moved, but we'd cross that bridge if and when needed.

I was determined to make this venture with Porter work, even if it took ten years. He had the contacts and it was up to me to land the first client to set the wheels in motion. While I worked on landing that first client, I also hit up all my retail contacts. I won some business, made some great trades, and things fell again for some reason.

I still received a monthly check from Jim and drove a company car. That wasn't enough, though. Money remained tight, something Tammy liked to remind me. Worse, I wasn't in a position to repay my parents. That bothered me more than bringing in just enough money to pay bills.

By fall 1991, I admitted something wasn't working. Splitting time between my retail business and my partnership with Jim didn't bring in the money I hoped.

On top of this, I stayed in touch with the contacts I made in Australia. The one ray of sunshine was the traders in our group of money managers performed well.

In August, Jim suggested I return to Australia. If things had been better I might have more open to the idea. With little money, I couldn't see how I could afford another trip, even if Jim paid for it, and how I could be away from the other business for a month.

Jim suggested this time I get a condo on Manly Beach for thirty days. I liked the idea of staying on the beach for a month. I racked my brain to see what else I could do to generate some cash. Even though I had studied, worked, and mingled in the white collar financial sector, I'd never been too proud to do whatever it took to make ends meet. I didn't mind going to back to doing something even at an auction, which could help my retail business. So after yet another fight with Tammy about money, I looked through the classified section. One ad in particular jumped out at me. Prime Time Handicappers sought people to cold call a list of known gamblers for ten hours a week at $10 an hour. That came out to an extra $400 a month and sounded fun.

Back then, 900 numbers were hotter than the surface of the sun. I called the number and the next day met with Tim Waldron, the owner. Tim, a lanky, slightly balding, congenial guy, apparently lived, ate and breathed college sports and gambling. He hired me on the spot and handed me a page with a call script on it.

I sat at a table—a plain old card table—to make my first call. Not ideal in a sub-level apartment. But if I made money, I wouldn't care if I sat in the middle of a lake on a floating chair to make my first call. One sentence in and I threw away the script. I couldn't follow that comical nonsense. Instead, I listened to what the client was most into and asked them if they thought they could predict the next game. That was my hook. Anyone who follows college sports has an opinion about the next game. After two minutes, I had signed the guy up.

Tim was impressed, and this seemed too easy to me. I knew I could talk any gambler/ college sport enthusiast into placing one small bet.

During the second week Tim proposed a partnership. He offered that we split everything fifty-fifty. I think he thought I might leave and start my own business when I learned out to attract gamblers. It seemed a good move on his part because I knew how to sell something I believed in.

He gave me a list of serious gamblers, guys who had money. Tim wanted me to talk them into sending us $150 cash, overnighted by Western Union. I told him what I thought of his mental capacity.

"You're crazy if you think people will send us cash for picks."

"You'll see." He laughed. "Unless you've worked in Vegas, you have no idea how much money people are willing to drop on an event. With your charm, and my picks, they're going to be asking if they can send us much more than $150."

I shook my head. And he proved me right. Soon more guys than I can remember were sending $150 each week for our picks. With the new arrangement, I received $75. My goal was to get ten a week, which equated to $750 a week and $3,000 a month.

Over the next few months, Tim and I became great friends. By the time October rolled around, I considered skipping the trip to Australia. My inner voice reminded that while I enjoyed this job and the potential to make tens of thousands of dollars, the chance to make tens of millions enticed me more. So off to Australia I went.

Things were different this time, but pretty much the same. I couldn't get anyone to bite on the potential of futures trading. Everyone wanted someone else to sign on first before making a commitment. The meetings, like the first trip, appeared to go really well. Each company asked the same question: "Who do you have from Australia?"

I could only answer, "Nobody... yet."

I felt so close, but yet a galaxy away. Until a gentlemen approached after another disappointing meeting. He introduced himself as Vick and said he wanted to meet later. He told me, "I really like the idea of futures and believe there is a big market here in Australia." He also wanted to know with whom I'd met so far. I rattled off the names of the companies and individuals.

"Those are all the right players," he said. "But here's the thing about Sydney, there are a couple of people you just have to get in with. If you can sign these guys, the rest will follow."

I nodded and got out my binder and pen. Vick first mentioned Ricky Allstott, a young man who grew up fast and took over a large export company because of his father's sudden death. I scribbled furiously while Vick talked. He also mentioned Ricky took risks. I liked that. Just the kind of person I needed.

Next, Vick mentioned Kerry Packer. "He's the richest guy in Australia." I stopped writing while Vick continued. "Throwing a million dollars at something is peanuts to him."

I liked this opportunity more than they first guy he mentioned. The possibilities rolled through my mind like a cartoon character with dollar signs in his eyes. "What's in it for you?"

"Let's just agree that if, and when, you get this off the ground, perhaps I could be your point man here in Australia."

Sounded good to me, but wasn't my call. I'd have to run this by Jim. I saw the benefit of having someone here to meet with the locals on a regular basis and felt confident Jim would as well.

I met with Ricky Alstott the next day, and was shocked. Not only did he have one of the nicest offices I'd seen—gorgeous cherry wood adorned just about every inch of the office, with plush couches, and a supermodel secretary at the desk—he looked like he was just sixteen. I found out he was twenty-eight, just five years older than me.

We got down to brass tacks and Ricky said, "I like what I see but I need to track this for a while. In my business, I need to look out for my shareholders and they hold me accountable for every investment decision I make."

"I understand perfectly," I said. "It is the same way with our firm. I can give you extensive history of each of these traders. These guys are truly the cream of the crop, and these opportunities won't be here forever. Futures is exploding, and money managers are changing the game."

Ricky absorbed that for a minute. He had heard all the hype and hustle, but he seemed to know I truly believed what I said. He also knew we needed to land him to attract other clients.

"I must say, I do like the risk reduction aspect of these futures markets," he said. "Is it possible to meet any of your traders?"

"Of course, if your interest level is high enough." This was something I never thought of before but now I'd have to establish a better relationship with my traders.

I visited a few more companies, and by not staying with anyone this trip seemed faster and slower than the last one. I left knowing Ricky would be my first investor. I could tell he knew an opportunity when he saw one.

Again, I returned from Australia with hope. This time, though, I prayed that hope turned into reality at some point. I needed it to. But in the meantime, I went back to work with the gamblers.

During my time down under, a number of gamblers began relying on our picks. Energized from talking to all those huge Australian players, I turned just about every, single new name on the lists Tim gave me into a paying customer. Our picks were going through the roof as well. November turned out to be a record month for us. Around the first of December, I was able to do something I had dreamed about for years, being an international businessman. I especially wanted to do business in Australia.

I bought my dad a car. Since I lost my dad's life savings, he drove the same Lincoln Continental for four or five years. Dad put about 80,000 miles a year on his Continentals. He needed a car he could count on. The one he owned at this point totaled more than 500,000 miles. Not many cars, particularly in those days, lasted that long. And Dad's was about to give out.

After working the list of big players with Tim for a few months, I stopped by the used Lincoln dealer. I bought a champagne-colored car with low miles. My dad would love this. And he did. I beat the car salesman up a bit, threw down $8,000 cash, and drove the beauty off the lot.

A few hours later, I rolled down the driveway of my parents' farm. The look on his face was a priceless blend of trying to figure out who could be cruising into his driveway and admiration of the sweet Lincoln they drove. When he recognized me, he put his hand up to his mouth. I got out, hugged him, and handed him the keys.

I looked around the farm and opened a chasm in my heart that took years to fill. Pens needed a fresh coat of paint. The barn needed a few repairs on the roof. The landscaping around house wasn't in its usual pristine golf-course state. Inside, I noticed less food in the fridge and no pet projects for Mom. This only strengthened my resolve to repay the money so my parents could live comfortably again.

Chapter 19
SO CLOSE

T
wo things happened during late 1990 and early 1991 that led me to believe mounds of cash loomed in the near future. First, Tim and I killed it during the 1990 bowl season. We made more money selling sports picks in four weeks than I made all year in my other jobs combined. Second, a friendship with a guy name Squid, one of the brokers in Jim Howitzer's office, became a business partnership that made us game-changers in the trading market.

Squid was truly nothing short of a technical genius. He was a practicing broker, but his forte was computer programming. In 1990, digital trading did not exist until Squid and I developed a system I believe may have been the first of its kind.

With his programming genius, Squid created a system that replicated the manual process of analyzing trends over the previous ten years. After inputting the data we received results within seconds. The trick was being able to accommodate any outlying variables, for various scenarios.

I spent my days hunkered down with Squid, conceptualizing the inputs, researching, and giving deep thought to what the system should generate. We built a rough, working model and began tweaking. And tweaking, and tweaking. Ultimately, we "inputted" all the known technical signals of the current market, and the system would generate buy or sell signals, based on the projected market direction.

The final challenge was to "back test" it. If we provided inputs from market conditions for previous years, the system should be able to accurately forecast, the market conditions for the next year, which was also in the past for us so we could analyze the results for accuracy. After much tweaking, the system perfectly predicted a year's market.

"Can you believe what we have here?" I said.

Squid grinned. "Something that will make us a lot of money."

While working on this project with Squid, Tim's father died of a heart attack. This couldn't have come at a worse time for him. Tim and his father had been fighting over the past year. Neither seemed willing to let go of the argument. Now, Tim regretted not telling his father how much he loved him.

"I never got to tell him I was sorry," Tim said. "He has no idea much I love him."

My heart broke for him. "Oh buddy, he knows. A father is fully aware of how much his children love him. That's part of being a dad. And he loved you more than you could understand."

Tim stuttered through the rest of the conversation, and probably doesn't remember anything we talked about. His father's sudden death prompted me to call my dad and tell him how much I loved him. Dad seemed shocked, but glad, to hear from me. After numerous calls with bad news, he probably appreciated a positive one.

I checked on Tim often, but into August when college football starts, he wasn't able to focus on betting. I didn't push him. Each person grieves in their own way and for as long as they need. The last time we spoke I got off the phone knowing that was the end of the handicapping gig. A shame too. I enjoyed working with Tim. We were like two frat boys who found a niche and were milking it for all it was worth.

At that time, personal computers were becoming more widely available but software licensing was expensive and tedious. We decided to simply sell the computer generated forecasts. My job was marketing our results to brokers for a monthly fee for the signals. Squid was to tweak the system from information I got from clients. We agreed to split the profits fifty-fifty from all revenue.

During December 1990, I called brokers until my ear nearly fell off. Using my sales skills, I explained the development of the system, and how we tested— with perfect results. Business began lining up.

A couple of weeks after the funeral for Tim's dad, I got a break. A large broker in La Jolla, California, bought in. This company employed a high number of salesmen with access to a boatload of medium to large clients. He asked if we could customize the system to specifically trade $20,000 accounts. Squid made the necessary adjustments. The client loved the results and we received our first fat check.

I landed our first big client. For a few days, I puffed out my chest and walked with an extra bounce in my step. The system worked so well, and I called often enough with updates that I soon felt as though I was a part of their office.

That started the avalanche of business. Soon after I landed a big discount broker in Chicago. We received another nice monthly fee from this guy. He showed is appreciation of the results by flying me to Chicago to do a special television show about how oil, interest rates, and stocks were affected when Iraq invaded Kuwait.

Word was getting around about our system. Door flew open faster than a herd of stampeding cattle. I developed a relationship with an attractive anchor on a very successful business channel, Financial News Network. After schmoozing, sending flowers, and laying on every drop of charm I could muster, she invited me to give telephone interviews every other week. If business was good before, based on our system's reputation, after giving a three-minute interview on the commodities markets, our phones lit up. This happened often.

During all this craziness, I made two trips to Sydney. The trips cost a lot of money, but Jim knew we must stay in front of those guys. I'd been pushing a particular trader who had an outstanding twenty-year track record and managed more than two hundred million dollars. That much money, back then, was a huge chunk of the market. I talked him in to a 33-percent split, unheard of at the time, of the business I bagged in Australia. Their fee at the time was a 3-percent management fee of the trades. They also received 25-percent of the profits. If I raised millions, I'd receive one-third. The promise of that payday kept me motivated.

I visited with Colin and Jessica a few times, and spent a lot of time with Vick, my primary contact in Australia. On those two trips I became close to Vick's family as well. His wife Karen was a lovely, bubbly woman and his two daughters were fun and hilarious. I loved the family-oriented nature of my Australian friends, and it felt like home away from home for me. Vick felt good about the progress we were making with the Australian investors. With a good-sized dog in the fight, he worked his angles, and he was very good at it. I enjoyed having him as an ally. After my second visit, we still had yet to bag a client, but they were right there. I just knew it was coming.

When I returned to Colorado, I dove back into selling our forecasts. In fact, I was curious to see which would make me a millionaire first—the forecasting system, or my partnership with Porter. The day after I got back, I met with Squid to catch up. Something seemed off. I first sensed animosity when he greeted me with, "The globetrotting TV diva is back."

I then noticed he wouldn't reveal details of changes he made to the program. Weird changes I felt produced slightly off-signals. Changes made without my input, based on client requests. This was stuff I needed to know because selling the product fell on my shoulders. Hiding information from me was never an issue before, so his attitude blindsided me. I tried to push him for details of the changes, but he became snippy and clammed up. I dealt with his crappy attitude for a week or two. When my commission check was sizably short, I asked why.

He said he decided to keep a larger percentage because the program was "all him." I didn't agree, but knew I might punch him in the face if we talked right now. Instead, I suggested we meet later than night.

Before I went home, I decided to check the system. I ran a previous year's data through and compared the signals to what happened in the market the following year. It was off. That shouldn't have happened. I compared data with the live, functioning version of the program, not a beta or even alpha version.

These signals Squid put out were ones being used by our clients. Information that could screw up the buy or sell signals for trades. And that had the potential to sink the reputation I had worked so hard on selling. I printed out the numbers and went home to think.

I drove back to the office and found Squid at his desk. Before I could bring up the numbers, he said he should have the majority of the profits because he programmed the system. I tried my best—in a calm tone—to explain that without marketing, sales and business relationships, his program wouldn't generate any revenue. He made another comment about me just running around expensing lunches in fancy restaurants and flying around on his dime.

"Those expenses," I said with air quotes around the second word, "are returning huge dividends in paying clients. Or did you somehow miss the checks that come in from people who called because of the TV show and the deals I've inked at those so-called fancy restaurants?"

He crossed his arms. "I've put a ton of coding time into this program. It's my brainchild. It's my idea. Without the program, there are no lunches. There are no TV appearances. There are no checks."

"Is that so?" I said, dripping with sarcasm. "So you miraculously figured out the inputs and trends, with help from your fairy godmother? Or was it me that busted my hump to analyze, fine tune, test, and give you feedback?" He started to protest, but I cut him off. "Nor to mention, the hours I spend getting feedback from the clients. I'm not being a jerk Squid, but you are not a salesman. Your strengths are coding. Mine are selling the thing. Fifty-fifty. Without you, yes, there is no program. Without me, or any marketing person for that matter, there are no clients. Understand that."

His face flushed, but he kept his mouth shut. He owed me money, but I knew in his current frame of mind, I wouldn't get the money any time soon. The next day I learned I'd never get it back.

The next day I waited until mid-morning, told myself to be cool, and called his desk. I figured we could meet over lunch and work this out. When he didn't answer, I called his boss, Nick Howitzer, and learned Squid had been picked up for a DUI. After I hung up with Howitzer, I called my office phone. Squid had left a message: "Look man, I got picked up for a DUI last night. Long story, but the whole thing is ridiculous. I know we were supposed to talk today, but as you can guess, I'm slightly indisposed at the moment. I'm calling from an attorney's office. I have to use the rest of the funds in the account for a retainer. As soon as I get some rest, and get my head together, we can talk."

I stood there wondering how much a new phone cost. Not sure, I set the receiver down as easy as I could and walked outside. I stared up into the sky. A sky that for many held so much promise. But not for me. I could only think of one thing: so much potential ruined by an ego.

Chapter 20

THE END OF MY WORLD

fter Squid killed our opportunity of what could have been the first automated futures forecasting system, my train wreck of a life appeared headed toward another cliff. While still hopeful about Australia, Jim and I had lost a little bit of our original enthusiasm. I think he really thought his contacts would open their bank accounts to us. Yes, a little naïve. And the reality they weren't eroded our optimism.

Although I learned much about myself while pursuing these small gigs, everything seemed to fall apart before the big payday. My birth certificate proved my age was twenty-eight, but inside I felt like a weather-beaten sixty.

The next morning I sat on my sofa, alone in my house, and reflected on my life. Not low enough to put a gun in my mouth again, but still pretty bummed out by Squid's action. When he got his DUI straightened out, he lined up a few backers but no one used the system like before.

I took a little inventory of what I'd accomplished so far. The list didn't look good, particularly the last five years. I lost all of my parents' money, had been arrested and imprisoned, and been suckered from one trading scam into the next, and found myself stuck in a relationship with a woman whom I wanted to dump but couldn't. I needed Tammy to testify in my lawsuit against the city of Ponderosa. I know that sounds shallow. I felt more for her daughter Tabitha than I did for Tammy. Sad, but true.

I needed to be with someone who understood my dilemma. I called Jim and asked if he could meet me at O'Shea's.

"Sounds splendid old chap," he said. "How about lunch first? I'd even eat a haggis right now."

"I'm sure we can do better. You buying?"

"No son, our fairy godmother is buying. Of course I am you knucklehead." Jim had taken to some Americanisms with a fervor. I laughed at how "knuckle" sounded more like "nookle" in his northern English lilt.

We met, ate, played pool, and continued to dream big about the potential in Australia. None of that made me feel better. I headed home, still feeling pretty lousy. Tammy had left a message on the machine she planned to work late again. This played into my suspicions about why she often worked late at the hotel on the reservation desk, but at this point I didn't care.

I sat on the couch and again pondered my life. What a great way to spend the evening. In this state of mind, nothing else seemed better. I thought many of my experiences were rock bottom, only to discover they weren't. So, where was rock bottom? And how could I avoid slamming into it?

For the first time in a long—really long—time, I thought I might find the answer in church. My memories, and the belief somewhere in my heart that God still cared about me, was the only light I could find in the deep, dark tunnel of my life. I decided to drop by a church near the apartment and talk with a priest. I wasn't sure about what, but I knew the conversation might get me going in the right direction. Any direction would be better than the one where I was headed.

The next day a gruff, but pleasant, voice greeted me when I stopped by the church. A middle-aged priest sat behind his desk with paperwork piled high along the front. He invited me in and motioned to a chair facing his desk. A nameplate in front of me read: Father Leery.

"What brings you in today son?"

"I don't know," I stammered. "My life is so out of control. I don't know what to do or where to go." I unloaded for the next twenty minutes telling him into how I was trying to earn my parent's money back, how it wasn't working out, and explained everything about my predicament.

The only feedback or comments he offered were, "Have you considered changing this?" or "Have you communicated that?" I also twice caught him looking up at the clock on the wall.

While I talked, I expected a hallelujah moment, where everything became crystal clear, the heavens opened up, and the answer fluttered down in the form of a white dove. Well, that never happened. After talking for about another twenty minutes while irritated Father Leery kept looking at the clock, I stood. I thanked him and apologized for wasting his time. If I was unhappy when I walked in, I was downright depressed and dejected now.

"Have you ever had a strange dream?"

How in the heck did he know? I encountered Moses more than twenty years ago in a supernatural experience at age seven. That experience is still as vivid as the night it happened. My Moses encounter was the first of many supernatural events in my life, but certainly the most weighty.

The night of the dream an angel hovered above my bed, just slightly off to one side. I don't remember the flapping of wings, and the messenger had no distinct facial features that I can recall. What I do remember is the gentle, nurturing, almost feminine quality to the being. I wasn't afraid, but a little unnerved. The angel finally spoke and told me I had been chosen by God to ask one question that He'd answer. The angel asked if I was interested. Normally a timid child, I answered pretty quick in the affirmative. The angel said, "Come with me."

The angel took me over landscape, trees, and vegetation. At blinding speed we soared toward a mountain in the distance. When we reached it, the angel set me down in an area where I could stand. Alone.

From a distance, a bright light headed our way. Soon I could see this light was a person in a brilliant, white robe with white hair. Intuitively, I knew it was Moses. I can't remember if Moses was walked up or simply came toward me.

Eventually he stopped in front of me. He said I would not be permitted to speak directly to or visit with God. Instead, I was to tell Moses my question and he'd take it to the Almighty for an answer.

"What is your question?"

I blurted, "When will the world end?" I'm not sure if the question shocked Moses, but it did me.

Moses disappeared and soon returned. Without an expression on his face he said, "1992."

I woke up. I don't remember being transported back. I don't remember Moses leaving. I just woke up. I laid in bed, saturated in the lucidity of the experience, and I wondered why I asked that question. Of all the questions I could have asked, why that one?

My seven-year-old self believed the encounter happened. And I had no idea how to process it. Was it an apocalyptic warning? It certainly felt like I was supposed to do something with it. If I sounded the alarm, would everyone make fun of me? I chose to keep it to myself. This produced more anxiety. For years I pondered this experience and why that question.

I sensed Father Leery was about to give me the answer. I sat, eyes opened wide. "Yes, indeed I have. I had a vivid dream when I was just seven years old, but I have never told anyone about it."

"I specialize in interpreting dreams," he said. "If you share it with me, it might add some clarity to your life."

I hoped he wouldn't make a snide comment, or worse, yell at me to get out of his office. I told him the dream in all its weird, vivid detail, and waited for his response.

"Close your eyes and try to go back to the mountain. I need more information to give you my interpretation."

Unsure that I could, I hesitated before I closed my eyes. And I couldn't, no matter how hard I tried. I visualized the mountain. I visualized the angel. Nothing. I relaxed and let my mind go. Then the weirdest thing happened. A mental image of my hometown appeared. I tried to swing my thoughts back to the mountain, but this new image persisted. I shifted in the chair to ensure I was here and not off in la-la land.

"I can't go to the mountain," I said.

"Where are you?"

"I am back in my hometown, standing right between the church and my old grade school." Every vivid detail of each filled my mind.

Father Leery pressed me to tell him what I saw.

"The church is on my right. It's a bright, red brick building. The school is to my left and is a drab cement color." I paused. "Everything to the right is in color. Everything to the left is in black and white." My pulse quickened.

Father Leery spoke in a clear, nurturing voice. "What else do you see?"

"It's a bright sunny day to the right. It is dark and cloudy to the left." I stammered. "That's odd."

"What?"

"Storm clouds, big dark clouds, are coming and rain is on the way. The wind is picking up."

"Go on."

"The area to the left with the school just started rolling up like a carpet, or a scroll, and it's heading for me. If I don't get out of the way I will be run over by this storm. I am forced to move into the bright sunshine and color. It feels warm." I inhaled. "I'm looking back and it is still rolling up. I have to run up the steps to the church. I'm running up and going into the church." The vision stopped. My mind went black. I opened my eyes.

Father Leery looked like he'd seen a ghost. "You've just had one of the most spiritual experiences I have ever seen."

A little freaked out, I nodded.

"God's message to you is very clear. You must return to Him and the church, and everything will be fine."

"What does that mean?" I said. "What about 1992? What does all this vision have to do with my Moses experience?"

"I don't believe the world is going to end in 1992," he said. "But I do think it does pertain to you. Your world could end in 1992."

"Like I could die?"

"I don't know what it means. But I do believe if you don't return to God, the world as you know it is going to change. And it won't be for the better."

"No, I think I will continue to live my life and go about my business," I replied slowly. I didn't mean to disrespect him or his ability to interpret events. After the experience with Bill Black, I vowed to not live in fear. I assumed that is what Father Leery wanted and I wanted no part of it. I'd spent too many years living under extraordinary pressure. Not only from what happened with the money, but the trials and not wanting to disappoint my dad. I didn't know any other way than to keep matters in my own hands. Giving everything to God never occurred to me.

I left the church content my life would probably suck until I took my last breath. Then I got a little good news that buoyed my spirits for a brief time. Mom, Dad and my sister Nicole wanted to spend Christmas with me, Tammy, and Tabitha. I hurried to decorate the house—lights, tree, the whole shebang. We had an extra room that functioned as storage and guest room but everyone agreed my folks and sister would be more comfortable at a hotel. We arranged for them to swing by the apartment first, and I'd go with them to the hotel to help them get set up.

My glee plummeted the day my family arrived. After a warm greeting from my sister and mom, who wondered if I was eating, I noticed my dad could barely get out of his Continental. He picked up his left leg out of the car and placed it on the driveway. I raced around to help him before he did the same with the right leg. "What's wrong?"

"It's nothing. Think I just have a bladder infection is all."

"A bladder infection is no joke." I helped him up out of the car, much to his chagrin.

"I have these all the time, son. I'll just get some cranberry juice. I'll be right as rain in a day or two."

I looked at mom. She shrugged. My dad could be a stubborn one. No one stood a chance against him when he dug in his heels.

I gave them the long tour of our small apartment, and we hung out for about an hour or so. My dad seemed uncomfortable and we headed to the hotel sooner than we planned. We stopped at the grocery store on the way and I bought the biggest bottle of cranberry juice I could find.

When I arrived at the hotel, I was pleased to see it was very spacious and had a huge bed for my parents. Nicole was getting set up on the pull out couch in the living room, and a wave of excitement rushed through me. Tammy, of course, was at work, which made me happy. I hoped she stayed away for most of the weekend. I really just wanted to spend time with my family, without her competing with my family for my attention, or demanding some thing or another. Before I made sure their luggage was hauled up from the car, I poured my dad a big glass of cranberry juice. He chugged it. Then I poured him another. As we sat and caught up, he finished another three glasses. By the end of the third glass, he'd made two trips to the bathroom. Something didn't seem right.

Dad's discomfort cast a shadow over the holidays. He skipped seeing the lights around Black Spring, refused a trip to the ER, hobbled around, got up and sat gingerly, all the while suffering in silence. We all could see his pain, but after refusing to see a doctor, we knew not to mention any remedies other than the ineffective cranberry juice.

Much to my relief, when Tammy joined us, the fun and laughter didn't stop. My dad joked around with Tabitha, and my sister and mom fussed over her with makeup and hairdos. I wished my parents could stay forever after what turned out to be one of the best Christmases I could remember.

When they left, I said to my dad, "I haven't bugged you this entire visit, but you have to promise me you will get checked out when you get home."

He looked me in the eye and nodded.

That hurt more than arguing with me. His silence indicated he suffered more than he'd let on during his visit.

Two weeks later, I received a call from my mom about dad's visit to the doctor.

"It's cancer," she said, her voice shaky. "Prostate cancer."

Okay, where was rock bottom? It couldn't be that far away.

Chapter 21

DOUBLE WHAMMY

Nothing could've prepared me for my mom's words. My dad. Cancer. I never imagined I'd hear those words in my life. Even before age thirty, I learned many, many things happen in life that we never imagined. Despite all my trials so far, this was the worst.

I didn't know much about prostate cancer so I asked more questions than Mom probably wanted to answer. She assured me that with this type of cancer, the patient has a high chance of recovery. That offered a slight amount of relief.

Mom also said Dad didn't like his doctor in Glacier. Apparently the doctor gave Dad the harsh reality of the situation with the hope he'd be serious about treatment. He was, to an extent. Dad found a Mayo trained urologist in Meadow Grove, South Dakota, and elected to have this guy perform the surgery.

Life stopped for me. No more my anger and frustration toward Squid. No worrying about the lack of success with the partnership with Jim Porter. No more caring about Tammy's distant attitude. I only wanted to make myself available to my dad leading up to his surgery in March and however long he needed me after.

In March, a few weeks before Dad's surgery and carrying the guilt that I caused the stress which gave him cancer, I broke. My resolve splintered. I collapsed on my knees in the bedroom and buried my face in the sheets. I wailed for a long time like a mourning widow.

I couldn't let my dad down. Despite all I'd done, I just couldn't. I thought letting him down before might have driven me to insane actions. This time, I was certain it would. I was truly desperate.

Desperate to change.

I knew I'd broken a promise to God. After He delivered me from the trading nightmare, I kept living life on my terms. I remained in an adulterous relationship with Tammy. I still chased money. In the past, I justified my desire of both. Not anymore. How does one argue with the Creator? One can't. Well, we can, but anyone who has ever argued with God knows how that turns out.

"God, I'm so sorry." I sniffed. "I've let you down. I've made promises I haven't kept. I treated you like an afterthought." The guilt burned for a bit. "But I need help changing. I can't do it on my own. Please God, help my dad. Please help my family."

Eyes full of tears and a full sinus cavity, I begged, "Please, please God, send someone into my life to help me turn myself around. I've been in this horrible relationship for seven years, and I need someone who is a positive influence on me. Someone I can love, and who will love me for me. Please Lord, take care of Tabitha. She's a sweet innocent girl. I'm too weak Lord, to stand on my own. I not only need you, but I need an ally, a partner who will not only love You but help me love You like I should."

I had no idea where the last part came from. The prayer just rose up out of me. I looked up, and rubbed my eyes. I'd heard thanksgiving was always a good way to go with God, so I did. "Thank you God for helping me so much already."

After six years, I finally came clean about blowing off my promise to God. I felt lighter. Relieved. Better yet, I had hope about my dad and his condition, no matter what happened.

The day before Dad's surgery, I met the rest of the family in Meadow Grove. The reality of the situation hit me when I arrived at the hospital. This was my initial first-hand experience with his cancer. Up until now, I'd call my dad every day. But I had not seen him since Christmas.

Dad laid on his bed in the private room and appeared comfortable, in good spirits. The doctor in Glacier believed the cancer to be localized to the prostate. We made ourselves as comfortable as possible in the small room, after a while, my sisters and I decided to explore the hospital. We ended up in the cafeteria and found a phone on the wall. We called and harassed my dad until he and Mom joined us.

The entire family hadn't been together in a while. We enjoyed a fun dinner, as fun as one can have in a hospital. We chided each other and laughed, probably to the annoyance of the other diners. After dinner, my parents returned to Dad's room, and the kids checked into a nearby hotel.

The next day, my dad remained in good spirits. Mom and my sisters fretted a little. My mood fell somewhere in between. After the nurse's prepped Dad, the family escorted him to the OR doors. The butterflies set in and I kissed him on the cheek. He whispered, "I love you, Tiger."

I bit back the tears and nodded. My mom and sisters fought tears, and I assured them we didn't have anything to worry about. One of the nurses told us he could be in surgery for four to five hours because of the intricacy of the operation. She suggested we go eat breakfast.

We found a quaint egg-specialty place nearby clearly positioned to accommodate the hospital. We talked, but not in the jovial tone of last night. I ate only half of my food. Like the others, I wanted to return to the hospital as soon as I could.

We'd been gone about an hour when we returned. Imagine the shock when I saw the surgeon walking down the hall towards Dad's room. He carried a chart and handed it to a nurse when he made eye contact with me. When we reached earshot, he said, "Bring the family into the private room down the hall."

Oh my God. What is going on? My mom begged the doctor to tell us the news here in the hallway. I put my arm around her.

"This will just take a minute," he said. "I'll be there in a minute and will explain everything."

We filed into a small, sterile-looking area. My mom and sisters took the chairs around the table. I leaned against the wall behind my mom.

The doctor entered and I fired off the first question before he sat. "Where is my dad right now?"

"In recovery." He took time to look at each of us. "We're monitoring him while the anesthetic wears off."

"His surgery was a success?"

The doctor intertwined his fingers. "The initial tests led us to believe his cancer was localized. It was not. He has cancer throughout his body. We were unable to operate."

A veteran of giving bad news, he let the words hang in the air. He didn't need to say anything else.

I went up, up, up out of my body. I floated in a stark white hallway. When I looked down at me standing among my distraught family, my sisters grabbed my mother to keep her from collapsing. Mom's shoulders heaved.

A loud noise to my left pulled my focus from my family. A door. The slam rung in my ears. I looked for who might have closed the door. I stood alone. The same noise to my right reverberated in the hallway. I whirled in that direction. The same noise behind me. Again, very loud. I wanted to freak out. What was happening? Was I dying? I looked at my body. I still stood, not moving, near my family. A fourth door in front of me slammed shut.

Now I knew. My world as I knew it just ended. No more running in any direction from God. Only one way now. Up. To Him.

Responsibility for my father's death sentence bore heavy upon me. Unbearable. Then crushing. What would I do? What could I do?

I vaguely remember the doctor calling my name a few times. One of my sisters stared at me wide-eyed. When I fully returned from this out-of-body experience, I volunteered to tell my dad the news when he woke from the anesthesia. I thought I could spin it in a way to keep Dad upbeat. I failed. A look of fear spread across Dad's face, a look I'd never seen. Before I could explain radiation provided an excellent option, Dad said he wanted to be alone.

I left him alone in his room. I walked into the hallway crushed. Mom hugged me and suggested we get something to eat. About two hours later we returned and found Dad walking in the hallway.

"What are you doing?" I said.

"I'm fine," he said, pushing his IV pole. "I'm gonna beat this SOB. Just watch and see."

That's my dad. Still the toughest guy in the world. He could do anything he put his mind to, and if he said "I'm gonna beat this," he could do it. And I believed him. The memory of this became one of the biggest character anchors for me.

Tammy offered her consolation for Dad's prognosis, but it was somewhat distant and noncommittal. I soon found out why. She came to me one day and said she wanted to go for counseling. This took me by surprise. I felt bad for thinking she might have stepped out on our relationship. Apparently she wanted to change her life. I understood the feeling.

Tammy selected a female counselor in our area with a good reputation. She came home happy after the first two sessions. Things went south after that. Tammy became more distant. Counseling was supposed to help her become more open, not more distant except when she wanted to cut me down.

One day during a fight, she said, "You know most men get better looking as they age, but you're getting uglier."

Typical manipulative Tammy. She needed to cut me down to feel better about herself. I didn't fight back. I put my head down, determined to plow through until I could escape this madness.

A few days later while getting ready for work, she said, "The counselor wants to see us together this Wednesday. If you care about this relationship at all, you will be there."

"Fine," I said. "I have no problem with that." I wanted to ask the counselor a few questions about Tammy's 'progress.'

At the appointed time, we arrived at the counselor's office. The counselor, Sarah, asked Tammy to describe our relationship. I endured fifteen minutes of a verbal ravaging that took every ounce of restraint I possessed to keep my mouth shut. During this assault Tammy admitted she believed I ran around on her every chance I got.

"Tammy," Sarah said, "would you mind stepping out to the other room so I can discuss some of these issues with Steve in private?"

Tammy left and Sarah, who had been described as vindictive and biased, turned to me. I braced for the worst.

"What do you think of your relationship?"

After I told Sarah about the craziness of the relationship and my goal to live up to my end of the deal of helping raise Tabitha, Sarah asked about my family. I told her about growing up in Ponderosa and, without realizing it, I spilled my guts about the commodity trading. She listened until I realized I may have given crucial secrets to the enemy.

"You're really hurting over this, aren't you?" she said. "You have been for a long, long time."

She seemed sincere and compassionate, or was I being tricked? I went with sincere and compassionate. My floodgates burst open. Every hurt, everything I'd done wrong over the last ten years spilled out of my mouth like water going over a waterfall. All of it came out. How I hurt my parents, and my sisters, and my friends. How I let my dad down, and now he was diagnosed with terminal cancer. I shook. I sobbed. "I don't know how they will ever forgive me. How could they ever love me again?"

Twenty minutes and a box of tissues later, I slowed to a whimper. Drained, the weight I'd carried lifted, leaving me lighter than I'd been in years.

After Sarah called her in, Tammy returned. "What the hell is going on in here?"

"We discussed some things that may help us progress."

"Oh did he tell you that he lost everybody's money?"

Sarah struggled to close her mouth and looked at me. After all the abuse, I was grateful someone else saw Tammy's mean spirit.

Now, Tammy couldn't hold it in. "As a professional, you have to know he's just manipulating you to think everything is my fault. That's what cheaters do."

"Please sit down," Sarah urged.

"Hell no, I won't sit down," Tammy yelled, her rage building. "This isn't about him." She pointed at me.

"If you were an outsider looking in at this scene," Sarah said, "what would you think of your behavior right now?"

"Listen, I don't know what you're up to but if you can't see he's a dirty liar, then you're not nearly as good as I thought you were."

I almost laughed, but caught a calm that washed over Sarah's face. I knew Tammy was toast.

"Can't you see your outburst is giving me every reason to doubt your credibility?"

"You don't know what you're talking about."

Still in a calm voice, Sarah said, "Consider who is calm in the room and look who is not. We're trying to figure out what can be resolved in this relationship. That means taking accountability where necessary. Remember you approached me for help."

"Well, if I'd known you were a quack, I'd have run in the other direction."

I wanted to laugh. Shouting and threatening your counselor will never get them on your "side," which appeared Tammy's intent. Tammy had provided her own rope, tied the noose, and had now just obliged us by putting it over her neck and kicking out the stool.

"If you're unwilling to admit you're a major part of the problem, I don't think it is fruitful for us to keep seeing each other."

Tammy let loose with a few choice words and stormed out. I bid farewell to Sarah and walked out a free man. Then I saw Tammy, a devilish rage on her face, waiting in the car. I might have experienced the shortest freedom in history.

Chapter 22
HOPE SPRINGS ETERNAL

Tammy fired up the verbal assault machine when I got into the car. I didn't respond to a single comment. Not when she called me selfish for taking Sarah's side. Not when she accused me again of cheating. Not when she said, "don't you dare blame your dad dying on me."

On that one, I quit smiling, but I didn't say a word. I really wished she'd leave. I wished I could leave. I really wanted to at this point, more than ever. But I couldn't. Not with the trial in three months. I know it sounded selfish, and it was, but I didn't want to sink my chances of winning my court battle against the city of Ponderosa by breaking up with Tammy now.

So, I bit the bullet. I figured I could last three months after putting up with her crap for five years. The cracks in our relationship widened. Just three more months, I reminded myself on a daily basis. Tammy "took" more overtime shifts. She worked more weekends and often checked on "special groups." A few times, she came home after I went to bed. Yet, her pay never increased. This pretty much confirmed my suspicion about her extra-curricular activities. I only needed to catch her at this point to end this fiasco.

With my ten-year reunion the following weekend, I put my plan to catch her on hold. I didn't expect Tammy to go. But she did. I'm not sure why. I figured she'd stay in Black Spring with her "other" boyfriend. I'm sure I'd have had a better time without her. On the other hand, I relished the thought of people of Ponderosa seeing us together after the false accusations.

I arrived at the hotel on Wednesday and waited in the usual spot. When she didn't show after forty-five minutes, I left. Seething, I drove toward the exit. Seconds before I'd have been a free man, she ran from the hotel entrance, waving frantically. I stopped. And regretted it almost immediately.

She slid into the car. In a dreamy voice she said, "Let's have the best time together this weekend."

I snapped. How could someone who had been with someone else sit in my car and play the perfect cherub. "How stupid do you think I am? You don't think I know you were just cheating on me with someone else in there?" Her eyes widened while I continued. "Stay if you want to stay, but don't insult my intelligence, okay?"

She scooted away from me and leaned against the passenger door. "Nothing is going on with me," she said, looking at the carpet. "I told you, I wanted to come back with you." Her body language said it all. I shook my head and pulled off.

The drive to Ponderosa may have been the longest ten hours in my life. So close to being a free man. Oh, so close. When I pulled into my parent's driveway, I flashed back to the infamous night with Officer Alex Harris. How different would my life be right now if I'd let Tammy drive.

Tammy and I barely spoke during the trip, even when she and I spent time with my mom and dad. I think we all grew tired of her inappropriate jokes and odd comments. On the bright side, Dad looked a little better and in a lot less pain. Dad also opened up to me about a lot of things that he hadn't before. Vulnerable things, in a discrete way, but stuff that said I want to share all parts of my life with you now. Where my dad and I once talked only business, we now shared everything. Our joys, interests, and loves. More than a few times our eyes watered up when we realized how truly similar we were.

When I wasn't with Mom and Dad, I was with Shawn, Justin, usually at our old hangout, the VFW. The first night, I sat there, hanging out with my laughing and joking. I told them stories about Australia, Squid, and handicapping. I experienced a few moments of wishing I'd never left Ponderosa.

The rest of our long weekend was a wonderful rinse and repeat. I spent time with my folks in the daytime and the evenings with my friends. The night of the reunion, Tammy and I dressed in silence—she in a short, form-fitting dress that would surely turn heads and me in jeans and a polo shirt. We entered the VFW arm in arm, playing the role of happy couple to the hilt. A local DJ spun the best songs from our high school years.

Of course, the drinks flowed and the girls danced. Tammy jumped right in like she attended my high school. During a break in the music, I chatted with Shawn and Justin. Tammy walked away to replenish our liquids. Then I saw it while she walked back, drinks in her hands and a seductive smile on her face. She was completely wrong. Wrong for me. Wrong for my family. Wrong for my friends. Wrong for my life. I pitied her for a moment. Then repulsion took over. I knew in that moment I could not be with her another second longer than I needed to be. Only the impending trial, ironically here in Ponderosa, kept us together. After that, goodbye Tammy. Was it deceitful? I didn't think so. After all, she had been cheating on me for some time. The least she could do for me was to testify for me.

When we returned, the new lingerie, wearing perfume to work, and the lying became comical. It seemed she wanted to continue cheating on me while "maintaining" our relationship indefinitely. I was the security, and some other scumbag—I suspected her boss—was the good time.

One afternoon while Tammy worked, I hooked up a little device brokers use to ensure they get their telephone orders right. I plugged the phone line into the recorder and hid the device under the kitchen counter. This type of recorder activated whenever someone made or received a call. After the most relaxing nap I'd had in months, I heard the door open.

"Honey, I'm home," Tammy yelled.

Her voice sounded too sweet. I bounded up off the couch and said, "I'm headed to Kwik Way to get a few things. Want to come with?" I knew she wouldn't go.

"Oh no, you go ahead. I'm wiped. It's been a long week."

When I returned, I heard the shower running. Perfect. I checked the recorder. Tammy made or received a call. I pushed PLAY.

"Hey Ed, it's me. I just wanted to call and say Felicia knows all about us. She says we need to be more discreet."

Just what I needed. And it didn't take long. I tried to hide the joy in my voice when I called her into the kitchen. She bounded in wearing only a towel.

"Explain this to me?" I watched her expression while the recording played.

"I knew you were recording." She waved me off like it was a joke. "That's why I said all those things."

"Just stop." I stopped the machine. "You are a pathological liar." She began to protest and I cut her off. "It's over."

"Don't be ridiculous." She panicked, voice rising and arms flailing. "It's a JOKE."

Without emotion, I said, "It. Is. Over."

Tammy cried the most I'd seen her cry during our entire relationship. I was sure her tears were more for getting busted than for remorse. I could have been wrong, but it seemed that way to me. She sat on the couch and sobbed and sobbed. While she cried, I waited in the kitchen. When she realized I wasn't going to be placated, she came into the kitchen with red eyes, sniffing and trying her utmost for sympathy.

I wasn't cruel, but I wasn't falling for it. She had played me for a fool.

"Think about it. It's what you want too."

"No, it's not. I still care about us."

I stopped her blabbering with one quick look. Even if she cared emotionally, she murdered the relationship as soon as she started cheating on me. And who knows when the affair started. After listening to a few more desperate attempts at reconciling, I convinced Tammy that she'd be better off with someone else.

Drained and liberated, I slept on the couch. I covered myself with a thin blanket, closed my eyes and sighed.

"Thank you, Lord," I whispered. I'd never make the mistake of taking His handiwork for granted again. "Thank you, thank you, thank you."

A pure, warm, peaceful joy flowed over and through my being, almost like oil. I hadn't felt like this since I was a child. I felt truly free. I had hope again. I had forgotten how glorious hope was. I lay on our crummy couch, and basked in God's overwhelming peace. All I could think was I knew I had a future again.

The next morning, I called my sister Brooke in Los Angeles and told her everything.

"Get out of there now," she said. "Get another place, or come stay with us but leave immediately."

I hadn't considered moving, but I figured it might not be a bad idea. I really needed a break from Black Spring. From Tammy, from Porter, from all the memories I had here.

We said goodbye and hung up. I needed to break the news to Tabitha. After a shower, I drove to the school and signed her out. When they called her down to the office, she ran up to me with a surprised look on her face, and threw her arms around my neck. Gosh I loved her like my own daughter.

"I'm taking you to lunch," I said. "How does the Ponderosa sound?" I knew she loved Ponderosa because of the buffet where she could pick and choose whatever her whim fancied that day. The best part of course was the dessert bar. She could make her own sundae, with any flavor she wanted, and she treated the experience like she was a designer gourmet pastry chef.

During lunch, I broke the news. "I have to leave."

"I don't think you will, but you definitely should."

"Why do you think I should?" I asked, feeling like I was the vulnerable one at the table.

She shoved a big spoon of ice cream in her mouth. "Because mom lies to you all the time."

"I know she does. And that's why I'm leaving." I swallowed harder than I wanted. "You know it has nothing to do with you. In fact, you're the reason I've stayed for so long."

She looked down at the table and nodded. "You've said before you were going to leave, but you never do. You would really be happier if you did."

I could not believe that such a selfless, young individual could be such a complete one-eighty from a parent. "This time is different though. I have to leave."

She almost looked happy for me, but I could tell it began to sink in that I'd leave this time. After lunch, I dropped her back at school. I got out of the car and hugged her.

"Just remember, I will always love you, and you can call me anytime, no matter what. Okay?"

She nodded. "Love you too. Thanks for the great lunch." She wrapped her ten-year-old arms around me for the final time. When she reached the front door of the school, she looked back and waved. And just like that, she left my life. At least that's what I thought. Ten years later, she contacted me. She wanted closure, so we met for lunch and said our final goodbyes.

I went back to the apartment to make sure I didn't leave anything behind. Hard to believe that forty-eight hours ago I caught Tammy cheating and now I stood on the brink of being a free man. For the briefest of moments, I wondered why I didn't take this step years ago. I walked to the kitchen and heard a key slide into the lock on the front door. I groaned.

Tammy entered. "You're still here?"

"Yeah, I was just about to call a cab to the airport."

"Can we talk for a minute?"

Not now. I didn't have the energy being this close to being done with her. "There's nothing more to say."

"But—"

I held up a hand. I didn't want to hear any more lies.

"Can I at least drive you to the airport? We can talk a little on the way."

I weighed the options. Listen to her for twenty minutes and save money or spend the money and ride alone with my thoughts. I opted for the free ride. I guess as my last show of kindness to her. "Not a word about getting back together, okay?"

"Fine. I just wanted to go out on good terms."

If she wasn't a liar, I might have believed her. I looked around the apartment one last time to make sure everything of mine was either in storage or in my suitcase. I paused at Tabitha's room with the pretty little butterflies on the wall and a pink and purple comforter rumpled on the bed. I shook my head and fought back a tear.

"Okay, let's go," I said in my most stern voice.

Tammy spent the majority of the trip apologizing. She honored my request to not talk about getting back together. "I'm so, so sorry. I never meant to hurt you like I did. I promise. I was so stupid."

"Listen," I said, "it's all in the past. I forgive you, so forget about it. It's time for a new beginning for both of us." I studied her tear-streaked face for a moment. "I want you and Tabitha to have a wonderful life. If you want to do anything just make sure you take care of her. She's such a blessing, and a truly amazing kid. Honor that."

Tammy nodded. More tears streaked down her face. The internal battle between feeling sorry for her and enjoying the elation that I was done raged until I stared out the open window and watch the final visages of Black Spring disappeared from my life forever. A small Tammy kept quiet, and so did I. When she pulled up to the curb at the Black Spring airport, she tried to hug me. I pulled away and got out.

"Please," she said, sobbing.

I leaned against the window. "I truly hope you have a good life, Tammy." While her cries escalated into a wail, I patted the door, turned, and walked into the terminal.

Brooke, Tony, and my nieces—ages three and five—greeted me at LAX. This felt right. Unbridled from the burden of a bad relationship, I enjoyed the family, the often weird but wonderful sights of Los Angeles, and reconnecting with two girls I knew. Both were fun, but this was not the time to get into another relationship. I needed to unload more emotional baggage. Not only was it too soon for a relationship, but I also didn't know how long I'd stay in LA. My answer, I found out, lurked right around the corner.

Chapter 23

CURVEBALLS
AND FASTBALLS

L ife has funny way of throwing a person curve after curve after curve. Until that person knocks one out of the park. Then it's straight fast balls for a while. Not surprisingly, Tammy had a hand in the next two curves balls. While in Los Angeles, I called her and asked if she still planned to testify on my behalf in the lawsuit against Ponderosa.

She greeted me with a few silence and a sob. "I am so sorry for all the hurt I have caused you. I never meant to hurt you."

"Don't sweat it," I said, trying to stay positive and keep her focused. "That's all in the past now so let's just move on."

She sniffled.

"I really need to know you will show up to testify in the trial. My case is nothing without you."

"Of course I will be there," she said, her voice stronger. "I already told your lawyer that I would be."

"I just wanted to make sure your boyfriend didn't have a problem with you coming."

"He sure doesn't like the idea of us being around each other."

I gritted my teeth. Him of all people not trusting me. He's the one who imposed on another man's girlfriend. Outside of court, we don't have to see each other. We just stick with being friends"

"That's what I told him." Her voice sounded shaky again. "He's here, I gotta go."

She hung up. She seemed sincere about hurting me. I sensed she'd keep her word. For that, I was grateful.

I left Los Angeles with a myriad of emotions swirling inside me. Regret for not keeping me word with God. Sadness for losing my folks' money. Hope that I'd be vindicated when I beat the city of Ponderosa. Thankfulness for my sister Brooke encouraging me to end the relationship with Tammy.

The morning after I landed in Glacier, a Friday, I headed to my attorney's office—Roger O'Hannon. I wanted to stick with Sonny after he won the cases our earlier cases. Because the case was now a suit against the city of Ponderosa, Sonny had referred us to a big-shot buddy, a guy who was the best in the region at offensive lawsuits.

From the start, Roger said he'd never seen small-town shenanigans like this before. The situation came up again. He felt he didn't need to subpoena her because she gave her word to be there for me.

"Are you sure?" I squirmed in the leather chair in front of his desk.

"I spent a good deal of time with her on the phone going over testimony." He leaned back in his chair and folded his hands behind his head. "She assured me she'll be there."

I knew Tammy could be very convincing when it played in her favor. I even believed she would testify. Nonetheless, not having a subpoena made me nervous.

"Why don't you call her again?"

"Give me the phone."

He spun the handset around. I punched in her number at the hotel and hit the "speaker" button. The front desk connected me with her department. "Me again."

"You shouldn't call me at work."

"I'm sorry." I eyed Roger. "I'm here with my attorney. We want to know—""

"I told both of you I will be there." She sounded annoyed. "Now I gotta go." The line went dead.

"There you have it," said Roger. "We got nothing to worry about."

The weekend with my buddy Shawn and his girl spun by in a blur. My parents arrived Sunday night and checked into the same hotel. Dad looked tired from the drive, but overall appeared better than he was three months ago when I last saw him.

Monday morning, my parents and I walked into Roger's office. He did not look good.

"Tammy informed me five minutes ago she didn't get on the plane," Roger said. "Evidently her boyfriend was worried you two might hook up while she was here."

Great, just great. The person I needed the most just three me the biggest curve in my life. Without her, we didn't stand a chance. Roger thought otherwise, but I knew we were done. I sank into a leather chair and cried.

"We have her prior testimony and statements so it is possible we don't need her." Roger didn't sound convinced of his own statement.

I walked into the courtroom a beaten man. A number of questions rolled through my mind that began with the word "why." Why did I trust her to keep her word? Why didn't Roger have a subpoena ready? Why didn't I stay with her for just three more months? I didn't I pull the trigger? Why did I continually get suckered into bad business partnerships? Finally I tired of berating myself and zoned out during jury selection.

After jury selection, Roger called the dispatcher to testify, followed by my dad. He only called those two to the stand. Both gave methodical answers. The jury listened intently to their testimonies that showed an out of control small town lawyer and cop. We rested, without Tammy's testimony, and their attorney called me to the stand. He picked holes in the case—chipping away at my credibility and claiming this was my attempt to make up some of my parent's money I had lost. Next they jumped on Tammy's absence. I sat on the stand, looked at the jury and knew this was it. We're toast. Nothing we can say at this point will win this case.

They finished, and while we waited in the hallway, the opposing attorney approached with a settlement of zero dollars. No winners and no losers. Roger looked at me as if to say, "Might not be a bad idea."

"Nah, let it ride," I said. "I've wasted three-and-a-half years of my life waiting for justice and this sure ain't it."

Roger looked at the opposing counsel and shook his head.

Two nerve-wracking hours later, the bailiff called us back in. The lead juror stood up. "The jury finds the verdict in favor of the defendant. Nothing shall be awarded the plaintiff."

Then the judge spoke. "The jury has deliberated, however I have an amendment. The plaintiff is also ordered to pay the entire sum of the defendant's legal fees to date." He slammed the gavel and adjourned the court.

I couldn't even look over at my dad.

"That's outrageous," Roger said and put his hand on my shoulder. "We can file an appeal."

"I'm done with it all, Roger. I'm so used to losing, I'm not even surprised. In fact, I'm not even really that upset. That's just my life."

A loser again. How many times now? I couldn't remember. Wasn't sure that I wanted to know. On one hand, I felt disappointed the corrupt officials in the city of Ponderosa escaped accountability, but on the other hand, I was truly free. Free of Tammy, free of the trial, free of the past.

For three long years I had put up with unthinkable behavior from a woman. At any other time I wouldn't have thought twice about leaving her in the dust. I wondered if it wasn't some sort of spiritual apprehension. When I was ready to change, and truly cried out to God from my heart, things started happening. They weren't necessarily easy, but at that point, any change was something.

Right after the trial, a buddy, Frank Fernandez from LaJolla, California, called with a proposition. He had axed all of his brokers, shut down his firm, and was headed in a completely different direction. He too had whiffed the opportunity in the money management arena, and like me, was after the bigger money now. He wanted to set himself up as a manager of money managers.

He invited me to move to LaJolla and become his partner so we could "kill it together selling futures products."

I was all in. I asked for a couple of weeks to get everything properly sorted, and then I'd be on the road. In the meantime, Frank said he'd work on forging a relationship a giant discount broker out of Chicago to fund all of the operating costs.

The day I left Ponderosa, I called Frank. He didn't sound happy to hear from me.

"Listen, the clearing firm called me," said Frank. "They're insisting on sending their own people down here to help me out. But they said they want you to come to Chicago to meet with them."

"When did all this happen?"

"They called me yesterday afternoon. They want their own partner working with me."

How could this happen again? I wanted to scream but I was just too numb. Another business failure. And this one didn't even get off the ground. Worst of all, I was starting to believe I was a loser. Whatever happened though, I had to get the money back. Right now, my only option was going to Chicago. So that's what I planned to do.

When I mapped out the 1,300-mile trip, I saw I'd pass near where my high school buddy Shawn lived in Jordan, Iowa. I hadn't seen Shawn in since the high school reunion. A stop to see him would do me some good. Maybe I'd find myself gain. I certainly wasn't, despite my constants pleas to the Lord, finding 'ole Mathew in Ponderosa.

I ended up staying in Jordan longer than an overnight stay. Shawn introduced me to Larry, a commodity broker. Two hours after meeting him, he offered me an opportunity to set up some managed futures business if I committed to stay for six months.

"Are you serious?"

"Damn straight I am." He slid a napkin across the table and told me to write down a figure. "That will be your base. In addition, you will also get a piece of the clearing." He excused himself to go to the bathroom.

"He's legit," Shawn said. "He has a huge brokerage, does a ton of business, and is buying up farmland left and right. It's your decision but he is a big trader."

When Larry returned, I slid the napkin in his direction. He looked down and extended his hand. "Done."

My job was to get a trading program started for local farmers and ranchers that would function purely on technical analysis, in essence a non-digital throwback to what I did with Squid. Coming from a rancher family, I needed little time to build relationships with the farmers. Soon many were keen to give it a shot.

Larry and I grew close as well, and I began to truly value him as a friend. One day when we were alone in the office on a rare slow day, I opened up and shared the Bill Black experience with him.

"You do know the only way you're going to make it back is by trading, right?"

I knew he was right, but I also knew the risk was getting deeper in the hole. I wasn't sure I was ready to go big again. Larry knew how to do it. His account fluctuated a couple of hundred thousand dollars at a crack, so I saw the opportunity.

"Tell you what, when you're ready, I'm going to stake you some trading capital to get started again. I can see the trading fire in your eyes. You just need to get back on that horse, and emulate a few things I've learned over the years."

Larry was exactly what I needed. I fought back tears.

Most night, Shawn and I went out, just two guys hanging out. Sometimes his girlfriend joined us. I enjoyed being single. I focused on enjoying my time out without the need to constantly "hook up" or look for a girl. I didn't care one way or another if I met a girl.

One particular evening, we walked in a new place called Mickey's. Walking across the parking lot, we could hear the live band. Shawn opened the front door and volume of the music tripled. We rounded the corner to the lounge. Time slowed. The music faded away.

A tall, slender and graceful angel, with long, gorgeous, brunette locks, walked toward us. A glow emanated around her. For a second I wondered if she was real. Then I noticed the serving tray in her hand. Awesome, she works here.

I'd heard of love at first sight. I discovered that it's true. I believed God sent this woman to me and she'd be my wife. I jerked back to the moment and smiled. She smiled back and looked genuinely amused.

"Hello," she said and walked past me.

I returned the greeting and gazed at her while she walked to the bar. The silly high school love struck feeling surfaced. I had to do something. With Shawn following, I walked up to the bar. "You have the most beautiful eyes I have ever seen." Corny, I know. Sincere though.

"Well, thank you." She grabbed her drink order, gave me another little smile, and walked away.

I turned to Shawn. "I am head over heels in love."

"I can tell bro. But it's you and the two hundred other guys in this place."

With the music cranking and the dance floor full, Shawn caught me looking over at her again. "You're really taken with her, aren't you?"

"Bro, I'm going to marry her."

I waited almost a week to visit Mickey's again. I strolled in at 4:00 p.m. on Friday. My future wife stood behind the bar. Two college-age kids sat at the far end. I took a seat as far away from them as I could. I ordered a beer then asked, "What's your name?"

"Kathryn. What's yours?"

"Kathryn." Pretty name. "My name's Steve."

She smiled that wonderful smile again. My heart struggled with what to do—somersault, stop, swoon. I grinned at her.

One of college kids berated her for not making a mixed drink he wanted, even after reminding him that she was filling in while her boss ran an errand.

"Fellas, leave her alone," I said. "Maybe just go somewhere else."

And they did, leaving Kathryn and me alone. I apologized for the two guys. She said that sort of thing happened more often than one might think and thanked me for getting rid of them.

"Good thing I rode my shining, white stallion today."

She giggled, and we chatted about why I lived here and why she worked at Mickey's. She needed money to pay for her last semester of college where she'd earn a business degree in just three years.

A woman with drive. I liked that. Then I rambled about my past—about the bad relationship I endured for seven long years, the trading ups and downs, my dad's illness, and how it appeared things might be finally turning around for me.

She didn't run to the other end of the bar screaming. She listened, and even offered some encouraging words. I left a little while later knowing I was hopelessly in love.

I told Shawn about my good fortune. He laughed and suggested we try karaoke the next night. "I'm game," I said, not sure I could impress any woman with my singing. Didn't matter, I only wanted to see Kathryn.

The next night we walked in and I saw Kathryn right away. My lungs failed me. Her clothes didn't get my attention. Her eyes did. Those beautiful brown eyes. Shawn and I grabbed a spot at one of the high tables. She looked over at us and gave us a wave. I waved back and gave her yet another goofy grin.

"Stop," Shawn said. "You'll never get her with a stupid grin like that."

I couldn't help it. My heart did all kinds of crazy things when I looked at her.

On her way to our table she grabbed a bowl of fresh popped popcorn, and brought it to the table. "Man the popcorn smells good. I haven't eaten any lunch today." She set the bowl on the table.

"You should have called me," I said. "I would've brought you something."

"Lunch would have been very nice." She smiled. "How about a rain check?"

I drowned in those big beautiful eyes. "Just let me know when."

"Tomorrow noon. China Wok. Don't be late because I won't wait ten minutes."

"I won't be one second late."

Shawn and I endured some painful karaoke, but that didn't matter to me. I was busy counting down the minutes to my lunch date with an angel at China Wok.

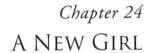

Chapter 24

A NEW GIRL

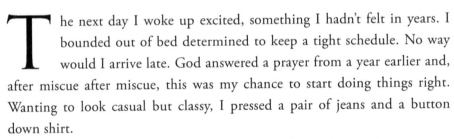

The next day I woke up excited, something I hadn't felt in years. I bounded out of bed determined to keep a tight schedule. No way would I arrive late. God answered a prayer from a year earlier and, after miscue after miscue, this was my chance to start doing things right. Wanting to look casual but classy, I pressed a pair of jeans and a button down shirt.

The countdown to noon slowed. Every second felt like ten. Every minute like twenty. At 11:30, I left in my Chrysler LeBaron and arrived at a Chinese restaurant at 11:45. I did it. Not late. I walked in and the unmistakable smell of Chinese food greeted me before the hostess. I looked around. No Kathryn. I'd earn points for this.

I checked my watched almost every minute. At noon, still no Kathryn. This didn't make sense. She seemed adamant I be here on time. How could she be late? I hope nothing happened.

I panicked and called the waiter over. "Is the only Chinese restaurant on this street?"

"China Wok is down the hill."

If I audibilized the scream in my head, I surely would have leveled the entire block. "Do you have a pay phone?"

He pointed toward the front lobby.

I grabbed the phone book handing from the metal chord, found the number for China Wok, and called. The hostess picked up and I asked for Kathryn. When she came to the phone I explained what happened.

"You've got five minutes," she said.

I made it in three. I entered another dimly lit Chinese restaurant. Kathryn's smile brightened the place. She laughed and shook her head as we made eye contact. She then gave me the best hug I'd ever felt in my life.

"You're off the hook buddy." She laughed. "For now."

I wiped my brow with an exaggerated "Whew." and we laughed.

Our three-hour lunch sped by much faster than my morning of waiting to meet my angel. Kathryn shared more about her family and her college courses. Every word that rolled out of her mouth captivated me. I enjoyed her company. She seemed to have her life together pretty well for something just twenty-two years old. At that age, I was on the verge of screwing up mine royally.

My heart soared higher. A movie of our life together started playing in my mind. Then she pulled the magic carpet out from under me.

"I have a boyfriend," she said in an unemotional tone.

I managed my best straight face while my heart sank into my shoes.

"However," she continued, "I am in the process of breaking up with him."

The magic carpet returned and my heart soared to greater heights. And I thanked God for this gift. "Is it not working out?"

"We're done. I need to make that very clear."

After the swing of emotions, Kathryn turned the attention to me. She wanted to know more about my relationship with Tammy, commodity losses, and the court case. Soon I was spilling the beans on everything. After all that, I figured she'd excuse herself and run back to her boyfriend.

"What's past is in the past," she said. "I honestly don't care about any of that. It's time now for a new beginning. That is what I am interested in."

I didn't have to explain my bad choices anymore. My girl wouldn't mock and demean me for the growing pains of my youth. Kathryn accepted me at face value. This was truly a new day. I didn't have a clue as to where this might end up, but I decided to trust God's direction for this relationship instead of imposing my will on it.

Afterwards, at her car, a small Nissan, she asked, "What are you doing tomorrow?"

She wasn't kidding about dumping the old boyfriend. I'm not sure when she planned to unhitch her wagon to him. Seemed soon, like maybe today.

"Would you want to go walking around the lake path around four?"

She wanted to see me again. "That'd be great." I smiled. "Should we meet at the entrance?"

"I'd like that," she said. She gave me a quick hug, got into her car, and drove off.

I jumped my car and headed back to the house. I envisioned vacations with Kathryn. I was careful to not dream too big. I decided to play it cool and focus on the friendship. Another first for me.

The next day, we walked around the lake. She wore my favorite perfume—Opium—again. The day after that we grabbed another bite to eat. The next day a milk shake. Apparently, the "boyfriend" was now an ex.

After three weeks we had become quite close, but still not an official couple. I wanted a kiss—without pushing it—to make it official. That happened one Sunday when she arrived at my apartment after leaving a family function to spend time with me. Something was definitely happening between us. Neither of us could deny it. Earlier that day, she stopped by before leaving to see her family. Now, here she stood, wide-eyed and grinning.

"Back already?" I said.

"I had enough of the family for one day."

My heart raced. This amazing, awesome, stunning, gorgeous—I ran out of adjectives in the moment—girl was as crazy about me as I was about her. I said I'd been thinking of her while I watched Chicago Bulls game. She raced me up the stairs and plopped into the easy chair nearest the television. We spent the rest of the game in a contest to see who could cheer on the Bulls the loudest.

During a commercial break, she asked, "Why is your detergent on the coffee table?"

"That's where I keep it now." I said, laughing.

She shook her head and rubbed her neck.

"Are you all right?"

"My neck is just a little strained from the drive."

"Come over here and I'll give you the world's best back rub." I prayed silently she wouldn't refuse.

"That sounds wonderful," she said and moved over to sit on the floor between my legs.

I gave her a neck and shoulder massage that a masseur would envy. She moaned softly a few times and told me how good it felt. After about fifteen minutes, my mind ran wild at the possibilities. I took a deep breath and prayed for anything but rejection. I put my arms around her shoulders and slowly pulled her into me. She willingly fell back into me. I just held her for a long time.

"Kathryn," I said, "I've wanted to ask you for a long time."

She looked up at me.

"May I kiss you?"

Without saying a word, she grabbed my face with both hands. We shared a passionate first kiss. I leaned back. Now we were a couple.

I don't remember much of the next few weeks. Kathryn and I spent more and more time together and talked on the phone a lot. Life was better now. The air cleaner. The grass more green. I smiled more. We lived in our little love bubble.

I soon understood why God put us together. Not only was Kathryn the most fun girl I'd ever met, she put God first in her life. She wasn't pushy about it, but it was clear she wouldn't sacrifice her time with God. She attended church every Saturday night. Naturally, I began going with her. Our ritual became attend church followed by dinner at Perkins. Her impact on my life was far deeper than the typical surface attraction.

Of course I wanted her to meet my parents, but hadn't met hers yet. I still called my dad every day and he commented often that I sounded happier than I'd been since probably high school. Mom said Dad lived in constant pain, but he never complained. I wouldn't expect anything less than him to suffer in silence. I wondered if I could suffer through cancer like that and not say a word.

I also worried that my parents might not like Kathryn. Mom sabotaged my relationship with Emily and neither liked Tammy. Would third time be a charm? I hoped so.

In April, we drove twelve hours to Ponderosa and arrived at 10:00 p.m. on a Friday night. Careful to not wake my parents, we unloaded quietly and headed out to the VFW. She took my hand during the walk. I looked forward to introducing my new girl to my friends tonight and my parents tomorrow.

Within minutes of our arrival, the kindness of my friends overwhelmed Kathryn. "I can't believe how generous everyone is," she said.

At closing time, it seemed a line of people hugged us and nearly everyone assured Kathryn that I didn't deserve her.

I awoke the next morning to the singing of a western meadowlark. Home, I thought. I rubbed my eyes and looked at the clock. A little before 9:00 a.m. I jumped out of bed and ran to the guest room where I tucked in Kathryn. I found an empty room. I bounded up the stairs and founded Kathryn with my father at the kitchen table. A coffee cup sat in front of each.

"How on earth did you trick this lovely girl into dating you?" my dad said.

"Good morning to you."

I kissed Kathryn, poured a cup of coffee, and joined them at the table.

"Seriously," Dad said, "how in the world?"

"I still have a few skills."

Kathryn snorted. "Oh, please. I had to ask him out on our first date."

While still laughing, my dad shifted gears and asked what she thought of the townsfolk.

"No disrespect to your town, but half of the people I met could be institutionalized," she said.

Dad's guffaw could be heard down at the town center, three miles away. He clapped his hands in glee. No one had ever made him laugh like this.

"Kathryn," he said, wiping his eyes. "I've always said we should fence off this town and charge admission."

He laughed harder, as did I with tears rolling down my face. Neither of my parents took to someone like that before. My dad absolutely loved Kathryn. His adoration of her confirmed my feelings for her.

We stayed in Ponderosa for a week and I promised to bring Kathryn back. We returned to Jordan, Iowa, so I could wrap up plans for my next trip to Australia. I wanted Kathryn to join me, but thought because of finals she'd decline. At least I could play the big shot and ask anyway. I knew she'd say no, but the request would make me look good when I offered to pay her way.

At dinner a few nights after we returned I popped a big question I wanted to ask for a few day. "I have something to ask you." Kathryn put her fork down, sensing this wasn't the usual "Wanna hang out tomorrow?" type of question.

"What's up?"

"I have to go to Australia on a business trip for thirty days in the early part of May. I was wondering if you'd like to go with me?"

"Sure." She jumped up and hugged me. "Sounds wonderful."

Wait, what? Did she just say yes? I couldn't breathe. In the same moment I was over the moon she wanted to go, but the airline and condo fees were a chunk of change. Could I even swing it?

"What about finals?" I thought this was my out.

"I am a good student and have a good relationship with all my professors. They'll let me take the tests before we go."

I smiled. Somehow, someway, I'd come up with the money. The heck with Disney World, I was going to Australia with Kathryn.

Chapter 25

A More
Enjoyable Path

I n the past, I looked forward to Australia for the business opportunities
and to get away from Tammy. This time, however, I faced a slight
dilemma. While excited Kathryn wanted to travel with me, I also knew
this was it for me. If I failed to land a client during this trip, I planned to tell
Jim Porter that I was done. Despite his enthusiasm for our potential, traveling
on his dime put a lot of pressure on me to produce. I've never been a quitter,
but enough is enough.

While I prepared for the trip, it dawned on me that Kathryn's go-getter,
never-give-up attitude had rubbed on me. I believed great things were about
to happen. In the past, I hoped they would. That shift gave me confidence,
something that in many ways outweighs hope by a large margin.

I also believed that when I cried out to God—and followed it through with
obedient action in breaking off the relationship with the person not meant for
me—He brought me Kathryn. Some may scoff at the notion and others may
believe God doesn't work that way. That's their choice.

God put her in my life at the perfect time, which is how He does things. She played a part in His grand plan to orchestrate my return to church, keep my moral compass pointed in the right direction, and for the first time in many, many years get my spirit, mind, and body in sync.

I worked out a plan for the trip to work for the first ten days, vacation with Kathryn when she arrived for two weeks, and work after she left. Jim, Kathryn, and my Aussie partner Vick Patterson supported my idea. "Land a deal," Jim encouraged me.

As usual, I landed in Sydney at 5:30 a.m., Vick picked me up, and while we ate breakfast, he regaled me with his desire to return to Candlestick Park in San Francisco to again see his hero Joe Montana. After my first visit to Australia, I learned to not make appointments the day I landed. I rested the remainder of the day.

The next day, I went after the big fish first—Ricky Alstott. I strutted into his officer early in the morning ready for my play. Power loves power, and I didn't disappoint. I over exaggerated the benefits and danced lightly on the risks. I closed with: "Respectfully, this is my last offer. If I don't close a deal with you today, I am moving on."

I meant it. The hours of flying back and forth to this continent, the endless meetings with Jim, the struggle to make ends meet, all of it came down to this. Paul looked down at the red carpet in his office for a few seconds, then up at me. "Mate, I don't trust many people in the world I trust intuitively." He smiled. "But you are one of them." He got up from his desk and sat in the chair next to me. "What I am going to do is give you a few million. Show me what you can do." He patted me on the shoulder. "You do well and I'll keep making that pot richer."

On the outside, I looked calm. Inside, the jumping beans of joy partied throughout my body. I was about to thank him when he added, "Take care of me. I trust you."

Trust. The words my dad said to me many, many years before. This time the words felt different. "You will be astounded at the returns I am going to get you." I put my hand on his. "You have my word I won't disappoint you. I truly appreciate the opportunity and trust you're placing in me."

Years of dreaming, and hard work, and keeping the faith finally paid off. I couldn't help but think Kathryn was my angel of blessing. She provided the motivation, and most importantly fulfillment within myself and God to have the confidence to display "a take it or leave it attitude." Now that I'd landed a client, I shifted my thoughts from landing the first one to growing the business. I loaded up the bases for the next nine days, and pitched American futures markets as if they were the last untapped gold mine on earth. The work from the previous trips put me in position to meet with the decision makers. And I hit 'em with everything I had.

I called Jim with the good news.

"That's my boy," he said. "I knew my faith in you would pay off."

One of my next perspective clients wanted to drop $50 million. Only if I thought we could handle that kind of money. We could. One of our traders had a great twenty-year track record dating back to his days of trading stock. He was managing more than $200 million at the time, a big sum for the futures industry. This client was close. I needed to land him too. I threw more bait in the water. "If it would help to meet the trader in person, I can arrange that to happen." He didn't bite, and never did sign with us.

During my first week and a half of meetings, every potential investor appeared impressed with the products and the track records of our traders. More importantly, with one of their own in the fold, they gave us more consideration than previous trips.

My confidence grew at each meeting, and I became a persuasive salesman. Because I believed in what I was selling, my "pitch" came across as natural and authentic. At the end of those ten days, I had one huge investor ready to go and four who'd watch, and when they met our trader, and their colleague performed well, they'd make the plunge. I could not have asked for more.

I earned the downtime with Kathryn, scheduled to begin the next day, a Monday. Vick volunteered to drive me to the airport at 5:30 a.m. to pick her up. "Glad to do it," he said. "I have selfish motives. I want to meet this woman who you can't stop talking about."

When she arrived, I lifted her off the ground in the biggest hug I could give her. She squealed, wrapped her arms around my neck, and gave me a kiss that told me she missed me. I put her down and introduced her to my "my good friend... er mate, Vick."

"Nice to meet you," she said, shaking his hand and flashing the smile I loved.

"Oh no, the pleasure is all mine I assure you." Vick gave me a sideways look and mouthed "wow."

If reality shows existed back then, our time together would have made for great television about two people heads over heels for each other. We enjoyed a romantic dinner at a different restaurant each night. I took Kathryn to the Opera House. Vick and his family showed us a number of beaches. I showed Kathryn the great outback and introduced her to a few local rancher friends. People were captivated by her beauty, and she wooed them with her charm. I often heard, "How did you convince her to date you?" or "Whenever you dump him, give me a call."

The highlight of her trip came on one of the last days. After seafood dinner, we noticed a big crowd in a conference room. With a number of Colorado Bulldogs having satisfied out thirst, we waltzed in. I introduced us to a group of brokers whom I recognized. We became an instant hit as the "funny Americans." The more we talked and laughed, the more people gravitated toward us. I knew enough names in the industry that I sounded like an insider of sorts and I happily dropped names, such as Alstott, which elicited a few "oohs" and "aahs."

An older lady approached and demanded to know who I was.

"Madam," I said, mixing my formal American with a fake Australian accents, "You may call me Steve and this is my lady Kathryn."

"I'm Elizabeth. I head up this institution." She glared at me. "You are drawing too much attention away from our employee party and I must ask you to leave."

"Dear Elizabeth, you have my word we will leave, since it would be terribly impolite to leave a half-full glass, I am going to finish my drink while you go over to that corner and grab our jackets."

Her eyes grew wide, she clenched her jaw, and for a moment I thought she might snap. "Fine." She snorted instead. She left to retrieve our jackets and laughter exploded from the group.

"Mate, do you have any idea who you were talking to?" one trader. "She is the CEO of this firm, which is the largest brokerage in Australia. Nobody talks to her like that. Nobody."

"Well, that used to be true."

The group roared again with laughter.

Lady Elizabeth returned with our jackets. I gave a big American hug and sincerely thanked her for her tremendous hospitality. I meant it, and she smiled.

Kathryn returned to the U.S. a few days later, and I went back to work. Instead of trying to sell more, I focused on bonding with these decision-makers. I wanted them to befriend me. From there, the investment would be a formality at the appropriate time.

When I flew home, I thanked God for the breaks. In less than a year, my life went from being a mess in every area to a life that I enjoyed. It now seemed inevitable I could finally pay back my parents, possibly in one or two lump sums, if my trader performed as he had for twenty years. I also decided I'd "retire" from plotting trades.

This meant I'd needed to resign my partnership with Larry Gallatin. I enjoyed the experience and his friendship. But this wasn't for me anymore. Sales or raising trading money was my new calling. I never quite understood why people said I was a great salesman, I was always just myself. Larry understood my change in plans and graciously allowed me to make good on my negative account down the road. Larry died before I could pay back the money, so I paid what I owed to his wife.

Kathryn liked my plan. Her approval was important to me I admired her motivation and ability to see things through. Next, we paid Jim a visit in Black Spring with a little side trip to see her parents. After taking Kathryn out of the country, I figured I should meet her parents. Her father—all six-foot-four, 260 pounds of him—reminded me of Robert DeNiro's character in *Meet the Parents*. But I survived and we headed to Black Spring.

We waited for Jim in Bambinos. He arrived with his typical huge greeting. "You did it, mate. Bloody hell, you did it," he said, lifting me off the floor in a hug.

"About time, eh?"

Jim spotted Kathryn and stopped. He looked me and back at her. "Blimey, how on earth did persuade this lovely creature to date you?"

Kathryn blushed, and I laughed. I introduced them and said to her, "This is the guy I have been telling you about."

"I've heard many stories about you," she said. "I'm really hoping they aren't all true."

"I am afraid they just might be," Jim said, feigning remorse.

Jim insisted on paying for the dinner, for which I was grateful. During the drive back to the hotel, Kathryn rained on my happiness. "I'm sorry I just don't like him. I don't think he can be trusted,"

My smile disappeared. "Are you serious?" I touched the brakes to avoid rear-ending the vehicle in front of us. "Can you form that strong an opinion so quickly?"

"I can't put my finger on any single thing. I just get a bad feeling about him. I hate to say it, but I really don't like him."

I didn't see that coming. And I worried about the dinner conversation the next night with Jim and Estelle at their home. The evening got off to a rough start when their hybrid wolves dashed and greeted us. The wild look to them concerned me.

"They new?" I called to Jim from the driveway.

"Yes," he said to me from the marble porch, then to them, "Get over here boys."

Kathryn was visibly startled, but didn't say anything.

After a wonderful dinner of Welsh Shepherd's Pie, Jim and I headed downstairs to talk in private. I eyed a leather wingback chair and sat.

"I've been working on a new design for the mining business," he said. "I have just perfected the prototype and I'm at the point where I need financial backing. This is where you come in. I want you to put together a business plan for us, and then you and I are going over to Australia to raise the money and start our own manufacturing business." I nodded while he sat and continued. "You will be an executive with the firm, and if—no when—we raise the investment cash, I will make you wealthy beyond your wildest dreams. And of course, you will still have all the time you need to run the money raising business. In fact, the two efforts may complement each other."

I knew Jim was a high-level pioneer in the uranium business. If he said he'd developed a new prototype, it was big, big news.

"You in?"

I didn't hesitate. "Of course."

He grabbed a calendar from his desk and looked it over. "I'd like this to be completed by the end of summer so we can head over to Oz by autumn and get this off the ground. Will that work?"

"Well, yeah." Very doable. That gave me three months. "If you get me all of the financials and background info I ask for, I will make it happen."

"You've met Dale French, right?" I nodded. "He will be your right hand man. Going forward, he is also part of the team as he knows the industry and the financials even better than I do."

I stood and shook Jim's hand to seal the deal. I hope Kathryn liked the deal and now Jim too.

Chapter 26

UP, DOWN—AGAIN

J im selected the name Porter Enrichment Enterprises for the new company. He made me an executive and gave me a seat on the Board of Directors. We set two goals for the first half of 1994: our "golden boy" money manager, Bob Poulin must have two outstanding first quarters and to develop the business plan for the new pump prototype. We needed the first to happen so when we returned to Australia in July we could show the fence-sitters how much they'd have made if they'd invested. The second needed done so we could show investors that they could make money in the uranium mining industry. This double-barrel approach gave us a chance to hit something.

For the trip, Jim took the business plan and company profile to a printer and made close to fifty copies. Meanwhile, Bob's trading topped 20-percent, an outrageous amount by today's standards. If a money manager can get 10-percent these days, he's doing extremely well. Bob's success created the illusion that our company knew how to make money, a great tool for leverage in negotiations.

We settled in to our seats in business class and Jim pulled out two spiral bound "business" books. He handed one to me. I leafed through the business plan section and admired my handiwork. I scanned through the company section—the list of proposed executives and renderings of the new pump.

I closed the book. "Didn't you say you needed my bio to include it in this packet?"

"Sorry, what's that mate?" Jim looked up from his book.

"Wasn't my bio as one of the proposed executives meant to be included?"

"It's not in there?" he asked, frowning over his bifocals.

"Must be a printer error. He did a fine job on the layout, but must have missed your bio page."

I wasn't sure what to make of it and gave Jim the benefit of the doubt. Yet, Kathryn's comment after first meeting Jim came to mind.

"Don't stress over it. I'll get it sorted as soon as we get back pal. These lads we're presenting to know you're on board anyway."

This time in Australia, we spent most of the time working and very little time playing. Jim and I wanted to land more clients for the trading business and investors for the pump. We meet with two or three companies every day for two weeks. I missed Kathryn, and longed for more time here with her. To make that happen, though, I needed to set up a plan to support us and our future. Jim and I talked about opening an office in Australia. We felt a local presence might allow us to sell full-time. While we had several investors lining up, some required a minimum of a two-year track record of earnings to cover their behinds. I didn't object. Anything to help them come onboard with us. When enough partners joined us, I could become a true manager of money managers. Then the big money would roll in.

When we talked about the pump, a number of Australians expressed interest. Mining was, and still is, a big part of the Australian economy. We landed enough investors to get Porter Enrichment Enterprises started with a bang.

Bob finished the fourth quarter of 1994 with gains of 28-percent, thanks to a steady market climb. All of us were making money—a lot of it. It seemed my worries were finally over. I worked on a plan to restore money to all the people I owed, Larry and my folks, and how long it would take. If we landed *the* big account, I'd pay everyone off within a year. How glorious. After all I put them through, to pay back within twelve months put an extra bounce in my step.

I seemed to have all I wanted. And more. God. Kathryn. Money. One Saturday in church, I experienced an overwhelming sense of goodness, love, and hope. Wisps of incense curled up through the cool air. Light streamed in through the stained glass. A wave of warm love washed over me. I sang along with the hymn. The tranquility of worship cleansed my soul like a gentle, ebbing river. Each week the worship washed away more of the scars of abusive relationships, the lies of failure, and, most of all, hopelessness. This particular Saturday, I felt as though my life spiraled upward.

I thought God had heard my cry to Him years ago. This day, I knew it for the first time. He rescued me. I knew it was Him. I worshipped quietly with a new level of humbleness in my heart. I looked up from my book, saw Kathryn singing and gave thanks for this angel.

During the first week of 1995 I spoke with Bob about my strategy for the foreseeable future. I wanted to guesstimate what I might be able to stash away for my parents. He thought the market was close to a major peak. Bob believed the market was poised for a major downturn and wanted to flip positions and ride the wave all the way down as well. Timing, of course, was critical. I called our investors. Pretty soon word got out and a number of companies wanted in, wanted the get a huge return on their investment like our current clients.

A week later, Bob started building in to a short position. At that time, the minimum leverage was zero and the maximum leverage was four times your capital. Over the next thirty days, Bob worked himself and all of our investors into a two-times leverage. This means if the market declined by 10-percent, we'd make 20-percent. Fairly straightforward numbers.

I trusted in and believed Bob implicitly. But because of the remaining psychological scars from the Bill Black disaster, I talked with Bob often about his plan. Each time I left, my head spun with excitement as he proved to me from years of trends, and graphs and bar charts, that we were about to go below the 1987 crash levels. I recalled that year painfully. Bob's goal positioned us and the investors in a fully leveraged position. When the market crashed, we'd make a killing.

"If the S&P 500 closes over 500, then I don't know my business," he said at one point during every meeting.

The S&P was trading around 475, a high number back in 1995, but an extremely low number at the time of writing this book. I thought the number might go up, indicating a very strong market. I didn't have the confidence, though, to question Bob's genius. He'd been doing this for decades with almost $250 million under management and, best of all, made our investors almost 30-percent in gains the previous year. So I hung tight and prepared to white-knuckle it until the market broke.

Then the market inched up to 480, 485, 490. Now we were down 12-percent. I called Bob in a panic.

I couldn't shake off the sick feeling in my stomach. He gave me another history lesson on wave counts, timing, and the like. "There has to be a time when you cut and run, right?"

"Of course, every trader has a stop point," he said.

"Is it 500?"

"Is what 500?"

"Oh my God, the stop point."

"Oh yeah man, don't worry about it. We're not going anywhere near there. You'll see. Just relax."

We were already "near that." The pain in my gut intensified.

The calls from investors began. Watching their gains in 1994 being whittled away made them unhappy and nervous. I reassured them with the lesson Bob taught me. Every investor said: "Keep your eye on things."

Oh, I was. I avoided thinking about how I'd react if we lost everything again. I forged these personal relationships and a responsibility to them. And right now I doubted Bob's judgment. Days, then week went by. I watched the markets with the same sick feeling I had when I was trapped in the cattle futures. Dear God, how did I end up here again?

My life went down the drain one day in late March. I flipped on the television at Kathryn's place near Minneapolis and found the financial channel. At the top of the hour, the beautiful blonde anchor said, "The S&P 500 closed over the magical 500 level on heavy volume today."

I called Bob. I didn't even let him greet me. I blurted, "We've got to yank it. We've got to reverse position. Or tell our investors to yank it all."

"What are you talking about?" Bob said. "Why are you hysterical?"

I sucked in a breath. "Listen, you said 500 was your stop point. The S&P closed over 500 today. We have to stop."

"I'm telling you," he said in his history lesson voice. "It's about to break. Now more so than ever. There is no way the market can carry that volume for so long."

"I've seen this before and I lost everything."

"No disrespect but this is a little different."

"How so?"

"I'm working by trends. Deep market analysis." I fiddled with the phone cord while he continued. "You simply didn't have that experience as a kid. And that guy was a shark. We both know it. I'm in this boat as well. I sure as heck don't want to lose my money. I'm telling you, it's not a science so I can't predict the day it's going to break, but it will. Any day now. Trust me."

I groaned. I'm sure Bob heard me. I didn't care. I hung up. I really didn't know—or understand—how I found myself in this position again. I remembered that every time Bill Black told me to reverse positions, the market flipped the other way. I didn't want to make that mistake again. I decided to ride it out.

By mid-April the S&P had shot up to 512. Kathryn spent many hours keeping me calm. I wanted to jump off a cliff. I wanted to punch Bob. I wanted to scream. None of that would help, and I knew it. Ten days later, the market corrected itself down to 505. That number proved critical for me. The market either topped out at that number or it was poised for a breakout. I decided if we went above 512, I'd consider that a breakout and I would be forced to get out and cut my losses—and everyone else's. Within days, the market breached my self-imposed cap.

I sat in my living room with my head in my hands. I wanted to cry but I wouldn't allow myself. I jumped when the phone rang. I answered. Ricky.

"What do you think, mate?"

I didn't hesitate. "Pull it all. It's time to cut our losses. I'll fax you the withdrawal papers and then you fax them direct to Bob. As soon as your positions are liquidated, your money will be wired back."

I hung up with Ricky, and, ironically, the money-managing business. If it hadn't been for the mining business venture with Jim, and Kathryn's support, I may have considered all lost. For about two weeks I brooded over the crashed money management business. Was life supposed to be this hard? I wanted to scream at myself. I saw the signs with Bob, but didn't push hard enough. I bought into the commitment that he believed the market would tank.

I also should have seen that pride kept him from pulling back. How could one man lose so many other rich men's money so quickly? Had I not said to pull their funds, the Australians would've lost a whole lot more than the millions they did. Still that didn't save my reputation. That market upswing shut me down for good with them. My hopes of quickly paying my parents back disappeared as well.

Chapter 27

LOSING MY HERO

With my dad's health failing and my chance of big money slipping away by the minute, I moved back to Black Spring, Colorado, and rented an apartment at the end of April. Without Kathryn. But with her blessing. She knew how much the debt weighed on me. I knew the people of Black Spring. I made a lot of money my first time there. Old memories of Tammy surfaced. I pushed them aside easily.

It seemed Dad was okay when I spoke to him on the phone every day. He refused to complain, which made it difficult to gauge how things really were.

My trades—for both me and my clients—were doing pretty well now. With each success, my reputation improved. I certainly needed that, after everything else I'd been through. I needed people to believe in me again. As a person first, a businessman second. Trading had become my bittersweet mistress. While I didn't truly love her, I needed her to get what I needed most—money.

As much as we could, Kathryn and I met halfway on weekends. With our fondness for small towns, we found North Altamonte, Nebraska, a place we grew to love. We stopped going to church. That bothered her. It did me, too, but seeing her on weekends kept me going through the dark times of being isolated and lonely. Yes, I was making money, but not fast enough to repay my debt. Within a couple of months I realized I couldn't be apart from her.

In September, when she moved from Jordan to Worthy, Minnesota, I left Black Spring to be with her. Worthy is located near the Canadian border. In the livestock business, I dealt with a number of Canadians. Being this close to the border might give me a great opportunity to work on some Canadian business. So I sold my business in Black Spring to a young couple who were new to trading.

Things clicked for me in Worthy. I got plugged into a well-known brokerage firm and began clearing my business through them. One day while Kathryn was in class, I took a lunch break and called my dad. He sounded frail. "You okay?" I said.

"I'm fine," he said. "Just a bit weary from the radiation and all."

He didn't sound okay. He sounded worse than I'd ever heard him. "Kat and I want to drive down and see you this weekend."

"Oh, wonderful. Your mom will be so happy too." And then typical of him, he changed the subject. "How are you liking Minnesota?"

"So far so good. I'm hoping to bag some of that Canadian business, eh."

He didn't even chuckle. Not a good sign.

"I look forward to seeing you. I was about to take a nap, so please don't mind if I jump off and talk to you tomorrow."

I stared at my desk until tears blurred my vision. I read a hundred harsh truths into that conversation. Our family prayed endless hours and countless prayers for Dad to go into remission. Apparently he didn't. I tried to convince myself that he was having a bad day. But fear took over. Friday couldn't arrive fast enough.

When we arrived at my parents, I saw the impact of his cancer—on both my parents. Mom looked as tired as he did. No wonder. She'd taken care of him in this progressively worsening state for almost five years at this point. Dad came to the door slowly. Kathryn chided him about this, telling him "we don't have all day." He laughed and grimaced a little. He hugged her tightly, and she wiped away the tears when Dad turned away. I looked away to avoid crying.

Despite his "I'm gonna lick this" attitude, I knew Dad didn't have much time left. Seeing your hero in a withered state sucks the life out of a person. No wonder Mom looked beaten down and worn out.

We spent most of the weekend indoors. Dad napped often. During those times, I talked with my mom and poked around the farm to see what had fallen into disrepair. Quite a bit, I discovered. The barn. The fence. Just about everything.

Kathryn and I promised to return the following weekend.

For the next three weeks, we fell into the same routine: leave Friday right after work, drive seven hours to my parents' home, and spend the weekend worrying about Dad's deteriorating health. I don't want to skim over that fact. A little part of me died each weekend when I first saw my dad. And then again when Kat and I left Sunday night.

Our prayers became more intense, fervent if you will, in our search for answers or remedies. It seemed God didn't hear us at the time as my dad looked worse and struggled more. I thought I'd been through dark times before but those times paled to this. Watching a loved one die could be worse than actually dying. A person feels hopeless, worthless. Yes, the trip took a lot of time each weekend, but I wasn't missing any opportunities to be with my dad.

I pushed the thought of the money to the back of my mind. Dwelling on it magnified my pain to the point of nearly breaking me. And that was the last thing my dad needed.

In early October, I missed a weekend because of several work-related matters. Kat also needed the time to focus on mid-term assignments. I called Dad, and he said not to worry.

"I'll be here next weekend," he said.

I sure hoped so. A pang of fear smacked me every time the phone rang that week. When Kat and I arrived as promised the next weekend, Mom and Dad were already in bed. Instead of going out, we went straight to bed. I feared what I might see the next morning. Those fears proved correct when I saw my dad.

I made an excuse that I forgot something and turned back before I greeted him. Kathryn walked right up and hugged him like nothing was wrong. I went outside. Mom followed. I needed a few minutes to accept what I had just seen. A weak, frail man. My dad. He looked like he aged ten years in the last two weeks. Mom said the pain meds didn't work, but still he never complained.

During breakfast, Dad talked about going to a big auction in the next couple of weeks. I guess that's how someone who is dying deals with the end of their life: they make plans for things in the near future. Dad took a nap after breakfast, and I asked Kat if I could be alone for a minute. I went to the bedroom and wept into the pillow.

For the next month or so, our lives revolved around the weekend trips. Kathryn and I tried to concentrate on school and work, but our thoughts were always on the next trip and how bad my dad might be. Each weekend we discovered that he'd gotten a little worse.

On Friday, near the end of October, Dad kept his word about attending an auction. Incredible. Despite his pain and failing health, he refused to stop working. He loved work. And in many ways, because of me, working was imperative.

Dad chose an auction in Tucker, Wyoming, where my sister Madison lived. Up until this particular day, he stopped by her house after the auction, ate lunch, and played with the grandkids. This day, however, Mom drove Dad to the auction. During the first few hours, he traded several loads of cattle at a huge discount. Madison arrived around noon with lunch she made at home and the three of them ate in the auction pen. Without warning, Dad's nose started to bleed. Actually, gushed, either from his condition or the medication. We're not sure. Mom and Madison couldn't get the bleeding stopped and led Dad to the men's room. While Madison stood guard outside the door, Mom took Dad inside. When he started screaming, Madison pounded on the door. He mumbled all was okay and he'd be out in a minute.

But he wasn't okay.

Because the cancer had spread to most of his renal system, Dad passed blood clots when he urinated. The pain became unbearable, even for him, a man who never complained.

When Dad exited the bathroom, Madison tried to maintain a brave face for him. "That's enough trading for one day," she told him. Her brave face gave way to fear that he might die in her arms. He looked pale, frail. Not the man we knew.

While she walked him to the car, she cried. Her fear turned to outright terror that he wouldn't recover from this episode. Her tears became heavy sobs. She got him settled and called me.

"I'm a wreck," she said. "You won't believe how bad Dad is."

"What happened?"

In between sobs, Madison told me. She also fixated on Dad wearing tennis shoes without the laces tied. His feet, she said, were swollen and he couldn't wear his cowboy boots. Dad without his expensive cowboy boots is like a bear without its fur. Dad was much worse than I thought. That's when my crying started.

"You need to get here right away," she said. "Dad is not well."

"I'm," my voice cracked, "on my way."

"Get here as fast as you can."

I cut quite a bit of time off the seven-hour trip. Despite what Madison told me on the phone, I wasn't prepared for his condition. Dad looked horrible. He looked frailer than I'd ever seen him, the life gone from his eyes.

Soon after I arrived, he admitted he needed help. He was in so much pain that he allowed us to take him to the hospital in nearby Newhaven to see if a doctor could dissolve the blood clots. No dice. The doctors tried. Nothing worked. All attempts at inserting a catheter failed. Dad's pain intensified.

The doctors at Newhaven called for an ambulance to take Dad sixty miles away to the town where his Mayo-trained doctor worked. While we waited, Dad sat on the bed in the ER in obvious pain. Deep crevices of pain appeared on his face. He asked if I could help him to the bathroom. I took him by the arm. Once tall and slender with a lot of energy, Dad shuffled when he walked. A few steps away from the bed, the blood clots broke loose. Blood, pain, and urine gushed onto the floor. Dad's face softened. I looked at amount of fluid on the floor and wondered how it was possible that much came out of him. Dad cried into my shoulder—I think from embarrassment—and said, "I can't believe that poor little girl has to clean this up."

Dad might have been stern at times. He might have been stoic. But his actions always spoke the loudest. Now, even with the angel of death waiting in the wings, Dad still thought of others.

I called the nurse. Another nurse joined her, and soon the floor and Dad were cleaned up. After we got him changed, I said, "This is a good thing." The relief on his face obvious, he still seemed more concerned about the nurses and what he put them through. I believe a person's true character is exposed in these types of situations. Dad shone like an angel.

We sat on the bed next to each other after they left. It was my turn to cry. "Dad, I'm so, so sorry for everything. I love you so much and I've put you guys through the ringer."

He lifted my chin. He looked tired. "What are talking about? What are you sorry for?"

"The commodity losses, the stress. Just everything you and Mom had to go through. I'm just so sorry." I sobbed like a baby now.

He put his arms—once strong and now frail—around me. I hugged him and he cried too. "You have nothing to be sorry for. That isn't the stuff that matters. What matters is that you're here with me now. You're a good boy. And I love you."

Those words opened the door to the prison where I kept my feelings. All the guilt, all the angst, all the worry escaped that night. My dad loved me. That mattered more than anything.

I held him and we cried together for several minutes. Madison and my mom soon returned. Within minutes, Dad had them laughing until they cried. I stood off to the side, taking it all in and being proud the wonderful person in that bed was my dad.

During the ambulance ride to the new hospital, I sat in the back with him. He looked worn out, frail. Like he had for much of the past ten years, he got emotional and sentimental. I guess that happens when a man gets older. He told me what he loved about my four sisters and me. He smiled when he explained how different we all were, but how he loved us individually because of our own unique little ways. He spoke as if he were reading the final pages of a long and wonderful book. I squeezed his hand and looked away to wipe away another stream of tears.

A few days later, the hospital put my dad in hospice. The blood clots returned and his doctor put him on morphine. What a relief for him, and us. Those who knew my dad—and not just his family—had a difficult time watching him decline. I felt hopeless to watch my father writhe in pain when the clots passed through his system. The morphine gave him relief, but Dad no longer remained lucid.

One day while I sat next to his bed, I remembered of a few previous conversations. He repeatedly said, "If anything ever happens to me, you make sure you take care of your mother."

"Of course I will," I said every time. And each time he nodded, knowing I'd keep my word.

I recalled the night I told him I wanted to marry Kathryn. I wanted him to know she helped turn my life around and I loved her.

"I think that's a very good move buddy." He smiled at me, the pride sparkling in his yes.

With morphine dripping into one arm and an IV into the other to dissolve the blood clots, I knew he'd never see that day. He'd never see our children. I bit my lip.

A day and a half later, with the whole family in his room, I got up to take a break and get some air. I leaned over the bed and gave him a hug. The emotional dam broke loose. I laid my head on his chest and sobbed. He put his arms around me and hugged me back. I cried harder. I heard my mother and sisters leave the room to give us a moment of privacy. Through sobs, I told him how much I loved him. He started crying and squeezed me, his tough cowboy mentality long since traded for a deeply caring and transparent demeanor. When I said everything I felt I wanted to say, I gave him one last squeeze, and left the room.

My sisters had formed a line in the hall with Madison at the front. What started out as a simple hug from me turned into a spontaneous, tearful goodbye to our dad. This was the moment the inevitable became reality for us. He led the way by accepting what loomed on the horizon, and now we did too.

Two days later, Dad slipped into a coma. Then the weirdness began. One night, with all of us present around his bed, my mother decided to go for a walk in the hallway. After she closed the door, Dad sat up. Wide-eyed, we looked at each other. "Kids you're going to see huge amounts of oil discovered on your mom's land. Make sure you never sell the land, or get rid of the mineral rights." Then he laid back down and was out.

He meant the small farm where he and I hunted that Mom and her sister had inherited. We're glad we didn't sell. The land sits atop the Baaken formation, a 200,000 square mile area. More than 7.4 billion barrels of oil have been discovered in the formation.

Another time, Dad sat up again, and scared us again. This time he called over Madison. "Don't do chemo," he said. And like the previous time, he laid down and was out. More than a decade later, Madison was diagnosed with breast cancer and underwent had a double mastectomy. She heeded his advice and did not do chemo.

As the week wore on, Dad slipped deeper into the coma. Communication with him ceased. We sensed he might be with us for only a few more days. We took shifts sitting with him. When not sitting with him, we headed back to a local hotel and rested. I'm not sure I could have made it without Kathryn. Before working at the bar where we met, she worked at a nursing home. She'd seen a lot, and her experience helped me deal with what me and the family experienced in Dad's last days.

November 10, Madison and I took the night shift. Dad tossed and turned more than usual. We left the comfort of the chairs and sat on opposite side of the bed. We tried to calm him, but he wasn't in the present. He kept reaching for the end of the bed and calling out, "Mama, mama," the name he called his mother.

Dad finally calmed down and we returned to the chairs. Then he tossed and turned again. This time he mumbled for a little bit like he was having a conversation with someone until in a clear voice he said, "Please forgive me."

His tone led me to believe he was talking with Jesus. During his life, Dad would make a comment about the "Big Guy upstairs," but he usually kept his faith to himself. I looked at Madison and we both felt a comfort knowing he was preparing himself spiritually to enter the next life.

In a surreal moment, and at a strange time with my dad about to pass away, God revealed a truth to me about my life. Dad had asked and received forgiveness. In that moment, at such a strange time, I remembered I still owed my dad a huge financial debt I hadn't repaid. Worse, my motivation was not to repay the money, but rather to win his approval.

This hit me hard and I wept. The Holy Spirit spoke to my heart, "Just as I have forgiven your dad, so has he forgiven you. And just as your dad has my approval, so do you have his. And more importantly Mine. You're free."

I wept—for my dad and because we were both being freed from our pain and bondage.

We knew his time was near. Our prayer changed to "Please take him, Lord." Dad lived through that night, his fifth straight in hospice.

Internally, my mind churned—about his pain, about what I learned from him, about what life looked like without him. I paced to keep my body moving, to ease the huge amount of stress weighing me down.

During the day, his breathing became more labored. We first heard the death rattle early in the evening. He was such a fighter until the end, never wanting to give up. I felt helpless seeing him in such anguish. I leaned into his right ear and whispered, "Dad, it's okay." He just kept fighting and fighting. "You can go now. Everything will be fine. I'll take care of mom. You just go on. Go be with Papa and Nana. You don't need to put up with this pain anymore."

He died less than a minute later.

We were holding hands when dad passed. Despite what felt like a bonding moment, I was completely numb. He celebrated his sixty-first birthday on August 26 and died November 12. He no longer suffered, and for that I thanked the Lord.

I looked over at my mom. A widow. Her husband of thirty-nine years gone to be with Jesus. I walked over and held her. I wanted her to know I would take care of her, no matter what. I pulled my sisters into the embrace and locked eyes with my Kathryn.

Now it was just us.

Chapter 28

THE AFTERMATH

My dad wasn't supposed to die. We'd been praying nonstop, and I'd truly been doing everything I could to pay them back, and prove I could be successful. That was supposed to be enough right? For God to hear me? It didn't even have to be quick, but He should have just fixed it. But He didn't. Now my world hung in a strange sort of limbo.

After Dad's death, Kathryn and I made a quick trip to Ponderosa. I lost my job while we were in Wyoming. I found out—via a fax—when we got back to Minnesota. I was too numb from my dad's death that it didn't matter. Exhausted, I slept for ten hours.

I woke up remembering an incident in high school. My dad firmly and unmistakably told me that a Meyers man was never, ever, ever to back down. A tough kid had cornered three of my friends and me for some reason. We stood facing the bully. We were afraid of him. This kid went down the line asking each of us if we wanted to fight. My first friend averted his eyes and said "no" in a quaky voice. The next one shook his head. The third one held up his palms and said, "No, man, no one wants to fight." While my buddies backed out, I picked up a large rock and was waiting for the bully to get to me. I shook a little. I'd decided to smash the rock as hard as I could into the bully's face. Then I'd finish him off. Whatever happened, I wouldn't back down. He stared at my friend with his hands up, sneered, turned, and walked off. He never asked me to fight. He couldn't have seen the rock. I held it behind my back. I dropped the rock to the ground. I really didn't want to hit him it. I might have killed him. I'd rather do that, though, than back down.

I felt the same way about my life. Dad's death wiped away the childish haze of living in a bit of denial while still hanging onto the hope of making billions. I decided I'd die before giving up. I didn't know how close I would come.

Part of the epiphany involved calling a firm in Memphis. This firm wanted me. Landing a job with them took off some of the pressure. I still had some retail work and the mining business with Jim. I explained that I needed to take care of some things with my dad's passing, and they were okay with that.

Kathryn and I headed back to Ponderosa for the funeral. Her comforting touches and soft words of love made me feel like I could face the funeral. An old family friend officiated the service. My sister Brooke and I gave the eulogy. I wanted people to know my dad. Yes, the townsfolk knew him from a business standpoint, but I wanted them to know how much of a brave, strong, and loving man he became. My mom, sisters, and I wrote the eulogy together. We ran out of paper trying to list all of my dad's remarkable characteristics.

The next day, at the Catholic Church in Ponderosa, I stood strong during the initial line of condolences. Old friends and relatives shared their best loved memories of my dad. I was strong when the priest began the ceremony with some comforting but heart-wrenching scriptures. I was even strong when Brooke and I started delivering the eulogy. Then I looked at my mom. She sat with Hannah, Lisa, and Madison. Yet, she looked small and alone.

Alone. In the big farmhouse. In the bed she shared with my dad. At the kitchen table every morning. At night watching television.

I wobbled in a moment of panic. Would she be okay?

Keeping a promise to my dad, I kept it together. We concluded the service with songs and prayers. Ranchers usually don't show much emotion, but I saw quite a few that day wiped their faces. My dad was loved more than I realized.

At the house, dozens of guests spent hours sharing stories about Dad. After we'd hugged the last friends and shaken the last hands, I approached Mom to discuss a short-term plan down for the farm. One way I handled grief was to deny it. Another was to focus on tasks. First up, getting the farm ready for my mom to sell it. She couldn't manage the place by herself. I knew it. In this state, I wasn't sure if she knew it.

She asked if we could deal with it the next day. I got it. Her mind was elsewhere. While she ambled off to bed—alone—I made a mental note of what I'd seen during the trip a few weeks before. I committed to coming back as much as could to work on things until spring. Then in the spring, I'd kick it into high gear and finish so we could sell in the summer.

The next day I made sure my mom had everything she'd need until our next trip back. My sisters did the same. She told us to stop fussing over her. Mom wanted to be strong and we allowed her. I think it was her way of coping.

During the drive back, I mentally went over everything I needed to do to keep my promise to dad, as well as make sure my mom would be okay. I had three irons in the proverbial fire, so I felt good about my prospects.

I hadn't heard from Jim Porter after my dad died, so I called the house the next day, a Monday. Estelle answered the phone. When I asked for Jim, she got snippy.

"He's in Australia setting up his company," she said.

His company. Really? "You mean our company? The one I laid out the business plan for and was supposed to be a partner in?"

"What must I tell you? Jim is setting up his company and he is going to employ whoever he sees fit." I really didn't like her tone now. "I can give you his number in Australia if you like."

I wanted to tell her to shove the number where the sun doesn't shine, but I thought better of it. "I'd like that number very much."

Without asking if I had a pen, she rattled off the number. Good thing I kept a pen and pad next to the phone. I hung up, seething. Not because he cut me out. More so because I thought he might do this. What a gutless coward. He couldn't even tell me himself.

I picked up the phone. And called Memphis. I needed to make some money, and fast.

For some, the arrival of spring stirred a young man's fancy. For me, spring meant long hours of painting, mending, and cleaning up. It was tough work at first. So much, more than I thought had fallen into disrepair. But after a little while I enjoyed seeing the progress when I completed a task, somewhat a poetic reminder of my childhood when my dad gave me chores on the farm.

I leaned against the fence after one particular day of hard labor. I looked toward the white clouds in the sky. And knew Dad was up there smiling down on my great work.

Another time, after a grueling day of fixing the feedlot, Mom asked me to sit after I cleaned up. "I have something for you," she said, patting the spot next to her on the bed. She held a little jewelry box in her hands. I sat and she handed it to me before I asked what was in the box.

Inside the box were two playoff tickets from the Vince Lombardi-coach era of the Green Bay Packers. I smiled. Dad treasured those tickets more than the tip clip and cuff links in the box. Next to the cuff links laid a little plastic band. I picked it up. My baby bracelet with my name, "Baby Meyers," date of birth, height and weight. He kept my baby bracelet. I wiped the corner of my eyes.

Since his death, I'd focused so much on the tasks at hand, I hadn't grieved. That changed when I saw the bracelet. I sobbed. Mom hugged me while the tears flowed unashamedly. I was one of Dad's treasures. He kept my bracelet. In those few minutes of crying, the hurt from his years of suffering and death evaporated.

That night I discussed finances with my mom. Dad's life insurance wasn't worth much, but the sale of the farm and equipment would be enough for Mom for a while. She asked about options with the money instead of putting it all in a savings account. I suggested Treasury Bills, T-Bills. Sold in denominations of $1,000 with maturities of one month, three months, or six months. T-Bills seemed like a surefire way for her to make some quick money with a 5-percent rate. I took $160,000 and bought three-month T-Bills.

I broke a promise to myself to never trade my parents' money again. Yet, Mom told me if I ever saw something good to go ahead. This seemed too good to be true. The firm in Memphis allowed me to use a portion of the T-Bills for margin, so against my better judgment, I played the sure thing on the cattle market.

Then the market tanked. How? How could a surefire opportunity not work out? The familiar feeling of drowning returned. I took a deep breath, liquidated some T-Bills to keep the cash margin up and told myself I would level back up. And never trade another cent of my parent's money in my life again.

The market didn't level up. The trades slide more and more each day. I was hemorrhaging my mom's cash. The $160,000 plummeted to $16,000 in just under three months. I stayed with the cattle futures instead of bouncing around. Often that will make the situation worse. I didn't say a word to Mom and she never asked. But after three months, she'd expect some interest. I sent her interest out of my pocket to keep things going.

What if she needed the money? What if she couldn't buy groceries?

Soon sleep eluded me, just like old times. Anxiety attacks returned, just like old times. Thoughts of worthlessness reminded me of my stupidity, just like old times.

I worried about what my sisters would think of me. Probably that they were related to the biggest loser they knew.

One night while I sat on the couch at home in Worthy, anger boiled in my stomach and spread to my arms, my heart, and my mind. I swore at Jim Porter's imaginary shape in the living room chair next to me.

"Gutless coward." I clenched my fist.

I moved onto Squid for wrecking the first computerized forecasting system.

"Idiot control freak." I clenched my fist tighter.

I went down the list: John Purger, Officer Alex Harris, Bill Black. Each name produced more anger until I couldn't sit any longer. I stood. A long silent voice whispered in my ear. *You deserve to die.*

Yup, I did. For this last transgression, I surely did. My mom was alone. I'd lost her money. I wept.

Do your family a favor. You know where the .38 is.

I thought of my bedroom nightstand. How could it have come to this? Dad was gone. I could see him soon, I reasoned. My sisters would do a better job of taking care of mom. If I grabbed the gun this time, Mom would bury her son and Kathryn would be a single woman again.

Chapter 29

FIXING ANOTHER MESS

I cried out to God. How did I end up in this situation again? Life, trading, everything was supposed to get better. Not worse. God knows I'd been trying. I eventually learned it's better to let God lead and not me. I still didn't trust God. I believed, but I believed only I could make things happens.

I hit my knees next. Next to the bed, I prayed with an intensity missing from my prayer time since I asked God for a good woman. "Heavenly Father, I messed up. Lord you know how much I cannot lose the rest of this money. God, please see my heart and know I am not an evil or bad person. I wanted to do the right thing. I may have gone about it the wrong way but God, please help me turn this around. Please Lord, I am begging you. Please."

I remained on my knees. A sense of quiet descended on me and I meditated on God's goodness, of all the jams He took care of, and His blessings.

At work, I went over my situation: out of the market with just $16,000 staring at me and no T-Bills. God please help me figure out a plan. I battled regret until He spoke. *Don't over-leverage. Don't overtrade. Be disciplined. Be patient. Don't ever, ever trade cattle again. Trade the charts that are giving a formation.*

With no other options, why not give this a shot.

The final instruction was simple. *Plan the trade and trade the plan.*

I bought five hogs with my first trade. Each went up $5.00 over two weeks, good for a $10,000 gain. Ten thousand down, only a hundred and thirty-four to go for mom. I didn't bother to think about the other money I owed. I focused on earning back Mom's money without telling here what was going on, a decision that kept her from a lot of headache and worry. I watched my dad suffer from a huge financial loss. I didn't want Mom to endure the same.

I worked the plan—making small, but wise trades based on the charts that were giving a formation. A chart formation is akin to a road map for a driver, but you complete it in your mind instead. Trade after trade paid off and I chipped away at the shortfall five thousand and then ten thousand dollars at a time. I cut the deficit in half in six weeks. A month and a half. I thanked God for what felt like, for the first time in my life, a good trading experience. Smiling, I wrote a check to my mom for her interest and put my head down to keep going.

One day, Kathryn said to me, "Honey, I can see a difference in you." She smiled. "I'm proud of you."

A little over two months later, using God's plan, I'd earned back the $160,000. Following God's plan was the key. No Porter safety net. No emotional dependence on a toxic relationship. Just hard work with His guidance and my obedience.

With new-found confidence, when the next T-Bill rollover came around, I talked Mom into putting $90,000 in T-Bills and speculating with $70,000 in her own account. I promised I wouldn't leverage much and would apportion spending money for her. She didn't hesitate when she said yes. The strategy paid move dividends and soon Mom's account swelled to $25,000 in the black.

Someone once said something about the older we get, the wiser we become. That may not be true for all, but for me, now in my early thirties, one lesson stood head and shoulders above the rest: forget God and things don't go well.

I respected my family's spiritual devotion, but I didn't live a super-religious life. Even when I leaned on God to get me through tough times, I went my own way after He got me out of a jam. We didn't host Bible studies in our home or anything like that, but my parents never compromised their confession of faith in Jesus Christ. This seed alone twice saved my life. Kathryn also played a huge role—one I cannot understate—in turning me toward God. She kept me in line. And after some of the stuff I did earlier in life, I needed that kind of person in my life. This may sound crazy, but those who have been madly in love, head over heels in love with someone, understand a man will do just about anything for the one he loves, including allowing that person to have an impact on their life.

In Worthy, I met several Canadians who wanted to trade one of two ways: as a hedger or a speculator. Hedgers want to minimize risk in their portfolio by using the futures markets to make a relatively safe bet on the future price of commodities, whether buying or selling. In essence, they create a financial "hedge" of safety for their portfolio. I helped a number of hedgers control risk with crops and livestock. Speculators, contrary to hedgers, are all about profit and use the futures markets to take risks. The investors like to speculate, hence the name, on the future price of commodities, usually with large sums of money.

My bank account grew, and I didn't have to split the money with a partner. Because I was being patient, trading with discipline instead of emotion, it was actually working. For the first time in my life, I felt secure as we rang in 1997.

One spring day, I drove to the jewelry store in Worthy. A rotund elderly gentleman greeted me over a pair of bifocals. His blonde assistant welcomed me with a smile. He asked me about my budget, which I said wasn't much of an issue. I said wanted the perfect stone and setting for "my soul mate." I explained generally what I was looking for. He nodded and led me over to glass box with an intimidating amount of sparkle.

I wondered if I hadn't overstated the minimal budget issue. Then I saw the ring—a stunning princess cut set in an intricate basket of eighteen-carat gold with two smaller, round stones on either side.

The stone mesmerized this relatively clueless male. I tried to hide my excitement, but the old man noticed. Without saying a word, he lifted the box from the case. "You'll travel far and wide and pay double to find a more beautiful piece than this."

"It certainly catches the eye."

"You haven't seen it entirely at work," he said, admiring the ring. "Victoria, my dear, if you will."

His assistant sauntered over with a pageant-worthy smile. He slid the ring on and she stretched out her slender hand, rocking it around ever so slightly so the large diamond scattered the halogen track lighting as brilliantly as a thousand fiery rainbows.

"I'm not sure." I wondered if he noticed me staring at the beautiful rock.

"This is what the piece is worth," he said, turning the box over. I feigned a heart attack and he chuckled. "Because a blind man could see your love is entirely true, I'll knock off 25-percent."

The number was a little above where I wanted to be.

"She's worth it my friend."

I felt guilty for finding a ring that quick so I stayed forty-five minutes looking around the store for future gift ideas for Kathryn.

I spent the next few weeks gathering photos taken during our four years together. Hard to believe we'd been together that long. At times, the day I met her seemed like yesterday. I put together a slideshow with the photos set to Queen's *You're My Best Friend*. I booked a reservation at a fancy restaurants a few towns over and hired got a limo.

The night arrived and I seemed a little too excitement when Kathryn talked in the limo about her classes. "What are you smiling at?"

"Oh, nothing," I said, snapping out of my daydream of things to come. "I'm just loving being with you tonight."

"Aren't you the sweetest guy in the world?" She squeezed my hand.

"I am quite a catch you know."

Fresh flowers adorned the white tablecloth at the intimate restaurant. We shared a light appetizer and recounted all our fun times together. I don't recall what I ate that night, but if the restaurant didn't already have at least one Michelin star, I'd certainly recommend them for one. When the waiter asked about dessert, Kat protested by saying we'd already eaten enough, but I asked if he recommended anything.

"The flourless chocolate and raspberry torte is simply outstanding sir, our signature desert," he said.

I knew Kat wouldn't resist. The waiter returned with a magnificent creation of chocolate and fresh raspberries and crimson syrup drizzled all over that covered half the plate.

"Goodness, it's huge," Kat said.

I motioned for Kathryn to dig in first. She smiled and plunged her fork into the wall of chocolate. Her forked smacked into something. Determined, she tried to dig deeper. She frowned until a sense of realization came over her. She dug around the edges, destroying the cake, and fished out a square box.

"Steve," she said, her voice trembling.

I scooted out my chair and dropped to one knee beside the table.

She opened the box, revealing her ring.

"My dear beloved, Kathryn, I love you with all my heart." I took her hand. "Would you do me the honor of becoming my wife forever and ever?"

A hush fell over the restaurant.

"Of course I will." She placed a hand on my face.

I kissed her and the place erupted in applause. A couple of gentlemen near our table shook my hand and congratulated us. During the ride home, I played the slideshow on the VCR. "My love," I said, "I want you to know that I will not just be your husband, but always your best friend. I promise you."

"Oh, Steve, thank you. This evening has been just perfect. I can't wait to tell my parents."

With her tucked under my arm in the back of the limo, I dwelt on the wonderful things in my life: Kathryn, a growing client base, paying off the debt from the Bill Black fiasco. Life couldn't have been better, with maybe the exception of my dad still being alive. I only wished I had found my feet sooner. Perhaps he wouldn't have succumbed to the cancer caused by stress. I tried not to dwell on it.

Soon after I proposed, the Red River, jammed up with huge sheets of melting ice, neared flood stage. Kat and I volunteered to help build a sandbag dyke forty-nine feet high, higher than the predicted estimate by the National Weather Service. The river crested at fifty-four feet and Worthy flooded.

The mayor ordered an evacuation. My office was downtown, near the river, and I lost all my paperwork, furniture and a good deal of electronic equipment.

We lived in a townhouse on the hill. We offered our home to a displaced family. Kathryn visited her parents in Colorado and I went to Ponderosa to regroup and formulate a plan. I also wanted to see my mom and fix anything that needed fixed so we could finally put the farm on the market.

After a week, I asked Kat if she wanted to live in Colorado.

"Not really," she said one night on the phone.

We needed to find another location. Going back to Worthy didn't make sense. At that volatile point in my career, I couldn't afford to let business drop off while the town rebuilt.

After her refusal, I thought of other options. Then I remembered Buffalo Jump in Wyoming where I stopped on the trip from Meadow Grove to be with Dad at his surgery. I remembered the town being clean and the people friendly. The next weekend, Kat and I spent a three-day weekend there. She loved the place, and we moved two weeks later. Despite having two degrees, one in business and the other in business aviation, Kat became my office manager. I opened my first real office in Buffalo Jump. In other locations, I worked from home or in an office.

My first client in Buffalo Jump was a cattle buyer and had actually heard of my dad. He handed me a check for $5,000 and said, "Now I don't ever want to trade S&Ps or anything like that." I turned his $5,000 into $10,000 and eventually $20,000.

One day a UPS guy strolled into the office. We chatted for a few minutes. Before he left, he pulled out his checkbook and wrote me a check for $100,000. Who writes $100,000 check to someone they just met? The next morning he returned and handed me another $100,000 check. We doubled his $200,000 over the next twelve months.

Kat and I worked hard for the next eighteen months, made friends with most of the people in town, and became a fixture in the community. I'd never experienced this level of happiness. Yet, something I couldn't put my finger on, didn't seem right. I pushed aside the feeling often and helped my love plan for our October 17, 1998 wedding.

Chapter 30

A LOVING FATHER

I n preparation for the wedding, Kathryn and I attended six months of marriage counseling at the Catholic Church we attended most every week. I thought "love would cover a multitude of sins," but I learned more about myself than anything else in those classes.

Our wedding weekend went off without a hitch. A number of my buddies from Ponderosa made the trip. Kathryn endured the groomsmen's dinner where she heard numerous tales of my childhood debauchery. A light snow covered the area Friday. Kathryn, of course, beamed when her father walked her down the aisle in the afternoon. I reminded myself to breathe. Family and friends clapped when I kissed her for the first time. Shawn chauffeured us to the reception in a red 1955 Chevy that I'd bought. The reception turned into the third "party" in three days, and became the biggest hit of all. Two years later, we took a delayed honeymoon to Italy.

Before we married, Kathryn and I found a three-story house on a wooded seven acres of land just a few miles out of town. The perfect place to unwind after a hectic day at the office. One day a few weeks after the wedding, I came home and called for Kat. No answer. Her Toyota Avalon sat in the driveway, so I expected her to be in the house. I looked in the kitchen, living room, and the master bedroom, calling for her along the way. With still no response, I bounded up the stairs to the guest bedrooms. I found her sitting on the bed in the first one, completely lost in her Bible.

"What are you up to?" I said.

"Oh hey." She looked up. "I picked up this faith walk book and wanted to read the Bible more."

Two waves of jealousy slammed into me. The first, I didn't want her to know God more than I did. The second, I didn't want to be left behind on a spiritual level. I didn't want to be like a few couples I knew that experienced problems because they were on different levels in their walk with God. But she was such a picture of grace and love, I just melted. I started out of the room so she could continue. I stopped. "Do you think I could borrow that faith walk book?"

She grinned "Sure and I'll pick one up for you too."

I walked downstairs feelings ashamed of my jealousy. More importantly, I knew from where it came. Despite all the times God rescued me, I still didn't spend much time getting to know Him better. I should have been the one leading.

The next week Kat gave me my own copy of the book. I dove in. During my studies, I learned that money had become an evil thing to me. The obsession with repaying my parents was like a junkie "chasing the dragon." I loathed money and its hold over me. But a desperate need for more remained strong. The problem with that mindset, just like the junkie, is you're always chasing a fast high. Nothing is focused and disciplined. Many traders will tell you when the real money becomes blurred with numbers on an account statement, and not respected, that eventually becomes a problem.

My mom's T-Bills must have been the final piece of the puzzle to bring that respect home. Money now became a tool, the numbers tangible. I harvested some profits, keep some back, and rewarded myself after profitable runs. I challenged myself with goals.

In the late nineties, tech and "dot-coms" propelled the market to new heights. Companies sank cash into ventures that promised to change the face of commerce by doing business online. Yet, cooler heads were skeptical.

In mid-1999, I recognized we were in a bubble, but still too dangerous to go in short. By March 2000, I felt the market had topped out. Too many Internet stocks traded at unbelievable levels with zero profits. I went short in a big way. For good measure, I rented a marquee sign outside my office to broadcast a message for the month of April. It said: "Stock Market Top In!"

This brought a lot of walk-ins. I begged each of them to get out of their stocks, whether they did business with me or not. Although many ended up trading with me, almost none sold their stocks. Numerous times I heard, "My broker says you're an idiot."

Being right wasn't important to me. I wanted to help them, but many didn't listen. It wasn't about being right for me, it was about helping people. Because of my history of messing up, I could see the pitfalls in the current market. Soon the NASDAQ tanked 90-percent and the S&P dropped fifty. We did well, but still left money on the table. One guy who didn't heed my warning went from a portfolio of $1.5 million to $87,000 in a two-year period. I knew what he felt like.

With my huge wins in trading, I felt I had the process down, spotting trends and making the right calls. More money rolled in. We took a few trips, but most of it went into the bank. In early 2001, my overall gains reached unprecedented levels. Sometime during the fall it dawned on me that my twenty-year high school reunion was nine months away. At the ten-year, I overheard the whispers of "rogue son" and "squandering his parent's money." This time, I'd show them. I set a goal to make a million dollars before the reunion.

I traded like a man possessed. Soon my tenacity paid off. For three months in a row I was up 100%. Kat seemed surprised, and impressed. Although she knew enough about the business and my past, she didn't say much, except this time. I heard the concern in her voice.

"How leveraged are you?" she said.

"I'm a little over-leveraged, but it's nothing I can't handle and escape very quickly. I'm up by so much it's worth a little risk."

Any good trader will tell you the fastest way to kill that kind of high is being over-leveraged. I broke my own rules and kept riding the huge wave. In the nine months leading up to the reunion, my earnings topped $1.5 million. I'd surely enjoy every minute of the reunion this time.

I did. I spent most of the time with Shawn, Justin, and Bear. We recounted our past shenanigans and participated in a few more. During the drive home while Kathryn slept, I questioned my happiness. Did I have what I wanted? A beautiful wife? Check. Countless blessing? Check. Financial security? Check. I truly thought making one million dollars would satisfy me. Instead, I felt tired, lonely, and empty. I chalked up this feeling to a bit of a letdown because most people at the reunion didn't care about my success. For a fleeting moment I wondered about dialing down my trading, but the thought quickly vanished as I knew I could double my last nine months earnings in six if I put my mind to it.

When we returned, I traded as aggressively as before. All my accounts went up again. One day during this unbelievable run, my first client in Buffalo Jump stopped by to celebrate his success.

"I just wanted to tell you how unbelievable this all is," Bill said. "And I wanted to say thank you."

I appreciated Bill's compliment. And the warning he didn't know he brought. This kind of visit usually signaled the top of a trading run had been reached. We chatted for a few hours. When I left, I knew I should liquidate everything the next day and chill for a while.

The next morning I went to work and decided not to liquidate. The main reason: laziness. A slide began the following day and wiped out my nine months of gain. I was trapped and burned out. I tried to survive in the haze, trading furiously to recover my losses. I'd forgotten my lesson of tangible money. And in this, God showed me another lesson to learn.

That night while Kat and I talked about what happened, the Lord's message became clear. He had answered all my cries for help but I'd done nothing for Him. Not a single thing. Yes, we attended church and gave when we felt like it. But we didn't tithe.

At one point, we said in unison, "We should have given away the money." Being in sync with Kat encouraged me. Yes, I messed up. Again. More importantly, we confirmed each other as being in sync with God. I had never before experienced that with anyone and it strengthened me to the point where I believed anything possible. We prayed together, and I vowed to God we would give 10-percent starting immediately.

After yet another great loss in trading, I recognized a pattern. I tried to convince myself slow and steady in the trades yielded better results. But I'd been successful with aggressive trading in the past when my motives were pure and my focus was on God.

I developed a daily ritual of reading the Bible and praying for a few minutes. Soon, I added other Christian books to my study time. The change in my life became dramatic. I enjoyed the most security and peace ever.

Trading seemed an afterthought. He honored my new commitment to life for Him by blessing us with whatever we need. Over the next few months I resorted to my disciplined strategy, but more importantly stuck to my promise to God.

I lost another huge amount of money, but the despair didn't overwhelm me like what I experienced in 1986. This time, I lived for the Lord, not me. I recognized I was a work-in-progress in the hands of a loving Father. He wasn't angry or disappointed.

After spending more and more time in devotions each day, I understood He knew when I slipped every time. That increased my love for Him, knowing that despite my drifting from time to time, He'd still love me.

One morning in 2003, I jumped into the shower, feeling great after praying and reading my Bible. While putting conditioner on my hair, I heard an audible voice. *He died for you, you know.*

"What?" I peeked over the top of the shower. Just me in the bathroom.

He died for you, you know.

The second comment triggered a vision in my mind's eye of Jesus on the cross. I fully understood what the cross signified. What He had done for me personally on the cross. I knew in that moment that if I were the only person ever born, and had sinned and strayed from Him, He still would have died to save me.

I stood in the streaming shower weeping like a baby. For the first time I finally got it. He died for me because He loved me—personally. Remorse for the pain I caused Him poured out of me with each sob. I vowed to never hurt my Savior like that again.

"I accept you Jesus." I wept. "You are my savior for I am nothing without you."

I'd called myself a Christian since childhood, attended church, and did all the "Christian" things one is supposed to do, but none of that prepared me for my true acceptance of Jesus Christ as my Lord and savior in the shower.

Over the new few months, Kat and I matured in our spiritual life and God continued to bless us. By the end of 2003, I'd made up what we lost. Sticking to our commitment, we gave large amounts of money to whoever in the church needed it. Nearly every day, I searched my heart for pure motives and repented for my many missteps and lack of follow through on God's call on my life. I thanked Him daily for my blessings.

Up to this point, Kathryn wouldn't discuss having children. I think she wanted me to grow up a little more, emotionally and spiritually. A birthday party invitation to a friend's house in April 2003 proved a turning point. During dinner our friend's half-brother to make a toast. His voice cracked, and he admitted his biggest regret was not having children with his girlfriend of thirty-five years.

I looked over at Kathryn, but she avoided eye contact. On the way home, we agreed it was time. "Let's pray about it and let's talk tomorrow," she said.

The next evening, she plopped down on the couch next to me. "I want us to be in agreement on how we're going to raise our child. I want us to be different parents. I want us to be godly and most of all, I don't want to be drinking parents. I want to stay at home and you will bring in the money. I want us to be the best parents we can be. If you can't handle any of this, then I love you more than you know, but I am simply not ready."

Okay. Not everything I expected. "All I have wanted since I met you was to be a family. I'd give up anything for that, especially things that have been distracting me from God anyway."

Her eyes sparkled, much like the night I proposed. I took her hand. We asked God to bless us with a baby and promised Him we would raise a godly child if He chose to bless us. A month later, she ran down the steps waving a pregnancy test. It showed one blue line and one red line. My beautiful wife was pregnant.

Chapter 31
GLORY BE TO GOD

Kathryn absolutely glowed during her pregnancy, her normal radiance magnified by the child growing within her. I accompanied her to every doctor's visit. I read all the highest-rated books so I could understand the stages of development.

We decided early in the pregnancy to avoid learning the sex of the baby. We figured this might heighten the excitement and keep us from planning the baby's life before it was born.

I talked to my baby every night. I'd always start with, "Hi baby. It's daddy." Then I'd tell the baby about my day, and how much mom and dad loved our kiddo. Sometimes I read a book or Scripture. Most time I just chatted. Kat said it felt like our child "quieted down" when I spoke.

We experienced one minor scare. During a doctor's visit in the second trimester, we were told the baby was laying breech. Kat's due date grew closer, but the baby remained breech. Kat didn't want a C-section so she researched options and discovered chiropractors can sometimes turn the baby with a hip adjustment. She contacted a chiropractor she knew and trusted, and scheduled an appointment. During the initial examination, the chiropractor assessed Kathryn's hips were out of alignment. We gave our approval for an adjustment. Kathryn laid on the table and the chiropractor moved her around into the correct position.

"Ready?" the chiropractor said.

"Yes." Kathryn sounded a little nervous.

The loud crack startled me. I looked at Kat. She waved me off, assuring me she was fine.

We went home and later that night the baby turned. Another instance of God taking care of us. Kat's little bump swelled to a round belly. I laughed, kissed her, and thanked the Lord for putting people around us with wisdom to help in these situations.

The next week we took advantage of a sunny afternoon for a stroll in the park. Part way into the walk, Kat grimaced and doubled over. I waited for the labor pain to pass before I urged her to grab our bags and head to the hospital. Kat wanted to wait a little to make sure the pains weren't false labor. Not long after we arrived home, Kat decided the labor was real and off we went to the hospital.

All the delivery rooms were filled so we were placed in a regular hospital room. Nurses hooked Kat up the necessary monitors. Soon the sound of our baby's heartbeat filled the room. Babump. Babump. I squeezed Kat's hand. The sound faded to practically nothing. We looked at each other, our eyes wide and our hearts pounding loud enough that we didn't need a monitor to hear them.

A nurse called for a doctor. The moments of waiting seemed like years. She rushed into the room and checked the monitor then turned her attention to Kat. Sweat formed on her brow. He prodded and probed. "It will be okay," he said. "The baby has a cord wrapped around its neck. We need to perform a C-section."

Kat cried and panic threatened to knock me down. With all that happened to me in the past, I feared how this might turn out. I said a silent prayer while the doctor made calls to the emergency delivery team. Right after he called, we heard the heartbeat start again, strong as ever. Kat looked up at the doctor with teary but hopeful eyes. I held my breath.

Our doctor arrived, checked a few vital signs, and prodded. "The heartbeat has gone back to normal. It's okay for now, but let's get this show on the road anyway."

"Thank you, Lord" I said out loud and Kat nodded. God taking care of us again.

Kat's pain increased. I'd never experienced this level of helplessness, even when I watched my dad pass away. Finally the doctor said, "Normally we can't do it at this stage but the anesthesiologist is here and we can give you an epidural if you want."

I looked over at Kat. "Might be a good idea."

Kat said, "I want to have this baby like God intended—numb from the waist down."

The room erupted in laughter. I've known very few people in my life who handle stress better than her. And in that moment, I knew she'd be the best mother on the planet.

The doctor walked Kat through what was about to happen. I held my breath and prayed. Sooner than I expected, I heard a cry. The cry of our baby. A boy. The doctor held him up for Kathryn and me to see. Based on family history, I was sure we'd have a little girl. I looked at my wife. Hair plastered against her skull. A tear-stained red face. Hospital gown dotted with patches of sweat. While I looked at her, my son's life flashed before eyes: us throwing ball together, wrestling, and spending time with him every free moment. Then I saw my baby bracelet that Dad saved. I understood exactly what he felt the day of my birth. I longed for Dad to be here. I looked back at Kat. The deepest love for my son's mom erupted in my chest. I hugged her while the nurses wiped our son off and suctioned his little mouth. Kat and I held each other and cried.

The doctor grabbed a pair of heavy-duty scissors and motioned to me. "Come on, dad. Will you do us the honors?"

I walked over and looked down at my baby boy. So much love, so much joy filled my heart. A nurse held him and placed the scissors on the umbilical cord for me. I cried, almost to the point of sobbing, when I cut the cord. The nurse smiled and turned to take him. I said, "Hey, baby."

People who have heard this story have said it's impossible, but my son turned his little head and looked up at me. I'm convinced he recognized my voice from all the talks we had for nine months. I nearly did a back flip in the hospital room.

I stayed the first night and our family slept in the same bed. With our baby snuggled between us, Kat and I acknowledged how much God had blessed us. We discussed living up to our agreement. Everything in my world seemed just right, and I intended to keep it that way with the Lord guiding me on my path. I knew our boy would be better than me. That thought filled me with great joy.

We named our son Luke. The day we took him home and I carried him into his room for the first time, I lost all ability to describe feelings or emotions. I could do two things: cry and thank God for His astounding blessings despite all of my prior shortcomings. His grace and love overwhelmed me.

At about four months, we introduced Luke to solid foods. Almost right away he experienced pain each time he ate. We took him to several doctors. Through the process of elimination, we discovered Luke could only eat six foods. His doctor made no guesses at how long it might take him to outgrow his food allergies, if ever. With God's healing he is slowly healing. From age two to four, he lived on grass-fed beef, potatoes, avocados, and squash.

As usual, Kat shone when the going got tough. She decided to sleep with him so she could nurse him around the clock and keep his immune system up. She also decided to eat only the foods Luke could tolerate.

To help her through this difficult time, I moved my office into the house. I'm glad I did. She needed my help more than I realized. Being home also gave me the opportunity to witness Luke's achievements: first crawl, first words, first steps. Every day I ate lunch with my family and took frequent breaks. I kept wanting to pinch myself. I'd never felt more this blessed or this happy. Ever.

During his toddler years, Luke kept us on our toes. Like most children, his curiosity about the world brought Kathryn and me much joy. I loved when that inquisitive look came across his face. We spent hours with Luke playing games, hanging out, goofing off, and answering his endless string of questions. His innocence and curiosity became a joy.

We enjoyed a stress-free home life, as much as one does with a young child in the house. Because, I believe, we focused on God. Our daily diligence kept our relationships with Him aflame. Kathryn and I read the Bible, as well as books on faith. I continued to read scripture to Luke. I cherished those times, my son sitting next to me while I read him God's word.

In our financial life, we kept our promise to tithe, to give consistently and generously. Trading was up and down at times, based on the fluctuation of the market, but that didn't keep us from remaining faithful in our tithing and offerings. Sometimes Kat picked a cause she felt led to give to. Sometimes I selected the cause. I loved the teamwork with her. Before we wrote each check, we prayed over it, and trusted God to do wonderful things. He never let us down.

In 2006, I prayed fervently for God to show me where He wanted His money to go. I wasn't hearing anything specific so I took a walk in the park one day during the fall. That usually cleared my mind. When I stopped the car, a flyer blew across the grass and it stuck to my shin. I peeled the leaflet off and glanced at it: a fundraiser in the park for a little boy who'd been recently diagnosed with severe medical issues. I shook my head, smiling at God's mysterious ways, and whispered "Thank you, Lord." I got back in my car, drove to the office, and wrote out a check. I drove back to the park, walked over to the fundraising pavilion, dropped the check into the donation box, and left. I walked away with a slight bounce in my step full of love and joy that God showed me where to give His money.

After that, my morning prayer became a plea to be used by Him. I laid face down on the floor and prayed, "God, I am all yours. Please use me this day." My personal prayers followed. Then I spent time reading His word.

I soon realized that if you beg God to use you, you'd better be ready. God may not always answer a prayer right away. When He does, things happen fast.

A few months later, a nice, long trading run gave us $40,000 to tithe. I prayed, "Heavenly Father, please show me today where you want your money to go." A pastor's face popped into my mind. I opened my eyes. I knew of him. We attended a different church. I shook it off, not sure we should give money to a church we didn't attend. I closed my eyes. His face popped into my mind. This happened a few more times. "Okay, okay Lord. I'll be obedient."

I gave up trying to pray, called his church, and made an appointment for the next day. I arrived for our appointment and we chatted for a few minutes before he asked, "What can I do for you?"

I didn't know where to start. He appeared to brace himself for some kind of morbid confession. "Pastor, you are going to think I'm crazy but here goes." He furrowed his brow and nodded, probably thinking the worst. I told him about my prayers, asking God where He wants His money to go, and the pastor's face popping into my head repeatedly.

The pastor's eyes widened. "Sit here," he said. "I'll be right back."

While he rushed off to wherever he went, I knew in my spirit I'd support whatever caused he brought. I wrote a $20,000 check and waited.

The pastor returned about a minute later carrying a folder. He laid it on the desk in front of me. "Go ahead." He nodded. "Open it."

I did and browsed over the first page. The folder contained plans for a free medical clinic in Buffalo Jump that would provide healthcare to the homeless, those on the poverty line, and single, unwed mothers struggling to take care of their children. I flipped through the next pages. My heart soared. The plan showed a long list of volunteers ready to help and blueprints for the construction. Only one thing was missing: money. I closed the folder.

The pastor looked less enthusiastic. "We're waiting on God. As you can see, we're ready. We're trusting God to provide the resources."

I sat, unable to move or talk. Tears flooded my eyes. God knew exactly where He wanted His money to go. In my obedience, He showed me. Very few things feel better than when a person gets out of God's way. His ways are always far better than ours.

"Are you okay?" the pastor said and explained the estimate of how many they could serve annually. To this day, I'd not seen that kind of passion from a person for a project.

I pulled out my checkbook from my back pocket and wrote another check for $20,000. I slid both checks across to the desk. "God has got you covered, my brother," I said, my voice cracking.

He stared at the check, then up at me. I stood up and hugged him. I thought we might cry. The presence of the Holy Spirit became strong and comforting.

Renovation of the building which would house the clinic began the spring of 2007. I thanked God for being part of the process. I witnessed His power from the beginning of the process for something desperately needed in our community. Being part of something that was right there on street level, helping the poor in one of the most fundamental ways is something that will change a man permanently.

I now understood one of the trickiest concepts in the Word of God, Luke 6:38: "Give and it will be given to you. Good measure, pressed down, shaken together, running over, will be put into your lap. For with the measure you use it will be measured back to you." When we give to God, no matter what, and with the pure motivation of building His kingdom, He blesses us far beyond anything we can imagine. I know that sounds cliché, but ask someone who lives by this principle and they will share stories that will leave your mouth hanging open.

Notice we weren't giving to be blessed, but giving out of a pure motivation of wanting to see the gospel spread. It didn't matter if we were blessed or not, we were still going to give. I believe this is the balanced way to approach tithing and giving. If you work to spread His kingdom, there is no way He won't ensure you have enough.

In early December, I stared out the window of my home office. A heavy snow covered the pine trees in the back. Branches bowed under the weight. Snow twinkled under a warm sun. I soaked in the marvel of God's work. The phone rang. I lifted the receiver from the cradle and greeted the caller. Mom's accountant.

"Just out of curiosity," he said, "I'm getting ready for year-end stuff and was wondering how your mom's stuff will turn out."

"I can answer that for you, but realize a lot can change in the last three weeks."

"Of course, I'm just trying to get an idea."

I put him on hold and looked up her account. Not bad. Sixty to eight thousand profit. Better return than I thought. I returned to the phone and relayed the numbers.

"Do you realize we're starting to pay taxes now," he said.

"No," I said, the wheels spinning in my mind.

Every year for twenty years we carried that loss forward. We could have carried it further if need be. A person is permitted to carry a loss forward indefinitely. Not us.

I hung up and leaned back in my chair. When he said those words, "Do you realize we're starting to pay taxes now?" Wow, just wow. I made their money back. That's when it hit me. Twenty years since I lost dad's fortune and eleven years since he died.

I learned a lot during those years, about money, about life, about love, about family, about me. Most of all, about God. God continued to love me and give me chance after chance, no matter how many times I screwed up. I think He allowed me to continue because He knew my heart. When I truly gave up myself to His ways, my life turn around.

I got out of way and watched Him do miraculous things, particularly in the area of finances. Not until I quit obsessing over money after my crash and turned over my finances to God, did I get out of way. I cannot stress that point enough. Too many times we get in the way of His plans and His ways.

We don't need to guide. Allowing Him to guide us reduces stress and increases our joy. Did I make the trades to earn back all my parents' money? Yes. Was I successful on my own? No. Only when God directed me did we see progress. To Him be the glory.

Always.

About the Authors

 Steve Meyers has been a registered commodities broker since 1987. He successfully predicted the tech stock bubble top in 2000 as well as the mortgage crisis in 2007-2008. He was featured in the PBS Frontline documentary, *The Six Billion Dollar Bet,* and has been quoted quoted in several leading financial publications, such as *The Wall Street Journal, The Motley Fool, Reuters, The Florida Sun Times.* Steve lives with his son in Naples, Florida.

 For more than thirty years, Larry J. Leech II has written and edited books, magazines, and daily newspapers. Larry teaches at numerous conferences nationwide and has become a much sought-after writing coach. Larry and his wife live in the Orlando area.

A free eBook edition is available with the purchase of this book.

To claim your free eBook edition:

1. Download the Shelfie app.
2. Write your name in upper case in the box.
3. Use the Shelfie app to submit a photo.
4. Download your eBook to any device.

Shelfie

A free eBook edition is available
with the purchase of this print book.

CLEARLY PRINT YOUR NAME ABOVE IN UPPER CASE

Instructions to claim your free eBook edition:
1. Download the Shelfie app for Android or iOS
2. Write your name in **UPPER CASE** above
3. Use the Shelfie app to submit a photo
4. Download your eBook to any device

Print & Digital Together Forever.

Snap a photo   Free eBook   Read anywhere

The Morgan James
Speakers Group

We connect Morgan James published
authors with live and online events
and audiences whom will benefit
from their expertise.